W9-ARC-531

LAWYERS AND MATRIMONIAL CASES

LAWYERS AND MATRIMONIAL CASES

A Study of Informal Pressures in Private Professional Practice

HUBERT J. O'GORMAN

THE FREE PRESS OF GLENCOE
COLLIER-MACMILLAN LIMITED, LONDON

COLLIER-MACMILLAN CANADA, LTD., TORONTO, ONTARIO

Library of Congress Catalog Card Number: 63-10652
Printed in the United States of America
DESIGNED BY ANDREW P. ZUTIS

For information, address:

THE FREE PRESS OF GLENCOE
A DIVISION OF THE MACMILLAN COMPANY
THE CROWELL-COLLIER PUBLISHING COMPANY
60 Fifth Avenue, New York 11, N.Y.

For Marion and Mark

FOREWORD

All apart from its vivid collective portrait of lawyers at work on matrimonial cases, chiefly cases of divorce and annulment, this book makes two distinct contributions to the sociology of the professions. The first is its detailed demonstration of what most of us vaguely know but often forget: like other professionals, lawyers are not all of a piece. Socially patterned variations of attitude, behavior, and outlook exist within this one profession just as they exist between the professions. Internal differentiation of this kind is probably most evident in the form of the established specialties, distinguishing the corporation lawyer, criminal lawyer and matrimonial lawyer just as it presumably does the surgeon, internist, and psychiatrist or the physicist, biologist, and economist. But, as Dr. O'Gorman goes on to show, marked and patterned differences of attitude and behavior occur even within one small sample of lawyers in one city engaged in dealing with one kind of case. This forces us to recognize that to speak of *the* lawyer, or *the* American lawyer, or *the* New York lawyer, or even *the* New York lawyer engaged in matrimonial cases is at best a gross approximation which invites the mistaken assumption that these lawyers comprise a reasonably homogeneous category.

In order to analyze rather than only describe the varieties of lawyers at work on matrimonial cases, Dr. O'Gorman distinguishes between lawyers engaged in general practice, in concentrated practice with some diversity of cases, and in truly specialized matrimonial practice. He finds that these several contexts of types of practice make for patterned differences in the professional behavior of lawyers as they handle matrimonial cases. Another type of context is provided by the distinctive orientations of lawyers toward their professional role: some are principally oriented toward the solving of legal problems, others toward their professional relations with clients, and still others toward money. Again, Dr. O'Gorman shows how these contexts of orientation are related to distinctive ways of dealing with similar kinds of matrimonial actions. Finally, in this short inventory of the internal differentiation among lawyers who have anything at all to do with such cases are the Counselors, who autonomously govern the relation to the client and seek an equitable solution to the problem, and the Advocates, who accommodate themselves to the client.

There is no need to set out here how these several types of lawyers variously deal with matrimonial cases, for Dr. O'Gorman does that himself, succinctly and with enviable clarity. But it should be said that he has begun to develop a prototype for future inquiries in the sociology of the professions which will examine the internal differentiation of each profession and establish the often complex differences of professional orientation and role-performance between diverse types of practitioners. What he has shown to be true of legal practitioners dealing with one kind of legal action presumably has its still-unknown counterparts within other divisions of legal practice and among the principal divisions of the other practicing professions—medicine, architecture, teaching, the ministry, engineering, and the like. This guide to internal differentiation, then, is one of the two major contributions of the book that reach beyond its manifest purpose of casting light upon a particular branch of legal practice.

Beyond this, the book provides an excellent specimen of sociological diagnosis. It draws upon a store of sociological knowledge to interpret observed behaviors as signs and symptoms of underlying social structures, processes, and functions. Throughout the greater part of the book, Dr. O'Gorman is the sociological diagnostician, who begins by examining the manifest facts of the case and then probes these further to provide tentative answers to the question: sociologically considered, what is going on here? Once alerted to this character of the book, the reader will soon identify for himself the major diagnoses Dr. O'Gorman draws from the evidence he has compiled, but it may nevertheless be useful to direct attention to a few of them.*

In one part of his diagnosis, Dr. O'Gorman sees current divorce procedures in New York as providing a research site strategic for investigating the familiar social pattern of "institutionalized evasions of institutional norms." He has a definite basis for describing the evasions of laws governing divorce in the state as *institutionalized:* they are patterned in a few well-defined types;

* Sociological diagnosis, like diagnosis in medical practice, must begin at the stage of assembling the data. Sociological interviews, for example, as was clearly the case with Dr. O'Gorman's interviews, must aim to elicit diagnostically significant data. For brief observations on such diagnostic orientations in interviewing, see R. K. Merton, M. Fiske, and P. L. Kendall, *The Focused Interview,* New York: The Free Press of Glencoe, 1956, pp. 18–19.

they are adopted by a majority of men and women seeking divorce rather than being scattered subterfuges privately and independently arrived at; to be effective, the evasions require an elaborate social machinery made up of tacitly cooperating clients, lawyers, judges, trained connivers and specialized creators of make-believe evidence of adultery; the evasive practices are widely known to depart from the letter and spirit of the law but, as Dr. O'Gorman's panel of lawyers testify, they are nevertheless condoned by officers of the court charged with implementing the law; and finally, the evasions are rarely punished, and when they are, they provide largely ceremonial occasions for reaffirming the sanctity of the law. These, then, are truly institutionalized evasions.

Dr. O'Gorman also reminds us that these evasions occur with varying frequency among the positions in the social structure occupied by the men and women seeking a divorce. In principle, the same law of course applies to all; it applies, for example, to rich and poor alike. But in practice, people variously located in the social structure scarcely have the same access to alternatives for securing divorces in full accord with the law of the state. For many of the comparatively poor, local subterfuges are functional equivalents of migratory divorces for many of the comparatively well-to-do. Different patterns of circumventing the divorce laws tend to be utilized by people of differing social status.

In this part of his sociological diagnosis, Dr. O'Gorman sees that evasions of the law governing divorce in New York comprise only a special and conspicuous case of the general social pattern of institutionalized evasions of institutional norms. The pattern develops whenever the laws governing a political jurisdiction or the formal rules governing an organization have lagged behind the changing interests, values, and wants of a substantial part of the underlying population. For a time, the evasions make the law tolerable, though hardly liked. They provide a cushioning effect for laws which are outmoded in the sense of being at odds with changing mores. In this restricted sense, the existence of Reno can be said to make for the persistence of severe divorce laws in New York. From this study it can be hazarded that if these laws were stringently enforced rather than liberally interpreted through legal casuistry and illegal connivance, the bottled-up pressures for divorce would probably make for a major change in the laws sooner than is apt to be the case under current conditions. However, should public testimony to these institutionalized evasions repeatedly occur, bringing out into the open the full extent of the gap between the principles of the law and the frequency of circumventory practices, this would also exert powerful pressure in its way for change of the law. Institutionalized evasions, it appears, tend to persist only so long as they are kept tacit. This means that "everyone knows" of the evasions in his private capacity but this severally known fact is not publicly, dramatically and repeatedly called to collective attention.

Another of Dr. O'Gorman's sociological diagnoses has implications that extend beyond his illuminating analysis of lawyers engaged in matrimonial actions. In this case also, he takes up a general sociological conception —a way of construing overt conformity to social norms —and applies it to clarify what he observes in his particular panel of lawyers. He recognizes that beyond the much-bruited question of the actual extent of behavioral conformity to norms is the further important question of the conditions that make for greater or less stress in living up to the norms. Not all overt conformity is of the same kind. In some cases, the social situation and the socialized personalities of those involved makes for ready conformity. But in other cases, behavioral conformity is achieved at the expense of particularly great effort. Just as William Martin found in his study of advanced medical students that under socially varying conditions differing degrees of effort to abide by norms of professional detachment are required, so Dr. O'Gorman shows us that the social and psychological attributes of matrimonial cases and the character of their practice subject many lawyers to acute stress in performing their professional role as it should be performed. His vivid account of this, chiefly in Chapter 5, does not resemble the standard portrait of the lawyer as cool and detached, assembling his evidence with technical skill, uncontaminated by emotional involvement. In the case of lawyers dealing with matrimonial clients, this image of the lawyer, based largely on normative expectations of what the professional man *should* do, is often far removed from what he actually does. For much more than these normative prescriptions of the profession enters into the concrete situation involving lawyer and client. Clients typically are anxious and under acute stress; they are often uncertain about their own wishes; they are often deeply hostile to their spouses, and, being themselves affectively involved, they often seek to seduce their lawyers into similar involvement with their cause. Dr. O'Gorman advances our understanding of role-conformity a considerable step forward by showing that the degrees of stress experienced by lawyers in conforming to their professional role varies with the kinds of legal practice in which they are engaged.

To interpret the complex feelings with which many of the lawyers in his sample confront matrimonial cases, Dr. O'Gorman employs the conception of sociological ambivalence to good advantage. This ambivalence is partly registered in the imagery reported by lawyers of the conflicting expectations, behavior, and attitudes of their matrimonial clients. As a frequent result, lawyers find their own behavior oscillating between detachment and affective involvement as they try to cope with their clients. Dr. O'Gorman's astute analysis of the principal sources of this complex of professional ambivalence provides another prototype for comparable investigations in other professions.

Of the many other general sociological ideas employed by Dr. O'Gorman in his diagnosis, I take note of only one: the self-fulfilling prophecy, in which initial faulty definitions of a situation so affect behavior as to produce results that are in ostensible accord with these prior definitions. Dr. O'Gorman finds that a substantial majority of his lawyers, especially among the type he has identified as Counselors rather than Advocates, are quick to reaffirm the professional norm that they *should* try to effect a reconciliation between client and spouse. But only a handful of these same practitioners believe that this normatively prescribed objective can be achieved in most cases. The prior conviction that marital conflicts are beyond repair once they are brought to the lawyer's office thus tends to subvert any serious effort to reconcile husband and wife. Dr. O'Gorman sees in this the pattern of the self-fulfilling prophecy in which this belief, inapplicable as it may be to a particular case, leads the lawyer to behave in such a way as to have that belief (sometimes misleadingly) confirmed by his experience. Persuaded that reconciliation is almost impossible, lawyers come to abandon in advance any serious effort at reconciliation and thus add a seemingly factual basis for their initial belief that it cannot be done. This cumulating evidence only reinforces the currency of the particular self-fulfilling prophecy.

There would have been reason enough for this book had it been confined to a lifelike portrait of a particular sector of legal practice. For my own part, I have found Dr. O'Gorman's book to be much more than that: a perceptive, lively, lucid, and instructive prototype for the sociological diagnosis of professional men at work.

ROBERT K. MERTON

Columbia University
June 1963

ACKNOWLEDGMENTS

In planning and doing this study, I received help from many sources. My general sociological obligation to Professor Robert K. Merton has been greatly increased by the patient and constructive criticism he furnished for the monograph presented here. Professor William J. Goode provided fruitful suggestions, for which I am deeply grateful. I am also thankful for the advice and encouragement offered by several members of the Columbia Law School faculty: Professors Walter Gellhorn, Harry Jones, Monrad Paulson, and Maurice Rosenberg.

In the initial stages of this research, I was aided considerably by the thoughtful comments of a number of lawyers. In particular, I want to acknowledge my debt to Milton M. Carrow and Richard Haydock. In addition, the following attorneys helped me to gain some preliminary insight into matrimonial practice: Mrs. Helen Buttenweiser, Merrill Clark, Donald Diamond, Alexander Lindey, Samuel Lovett, Morris Ploscowe, Leonard Rosenfeld, Judge Sylvia Singer, Howard H. Spellman, and Richard H. Wels.

The study could not have been carried out without the cooperation of the eighty-two lawyers in the sample. I am happy to acknowledge my heavy debt to these anonymous members of the legal profession, who interrupted their busy work schedules to be interviewed.

The data for the study were collected in 1957–1958. I am grateful for the award of a research training fellowship by the Social Science Research Council which gave me the opportunity to undertake this research.

Beyond these sources of help, I am deeply indebted to two men. Professor William C. Casey not only introduced me to the fascinating world of sociological ideas; he also taught me to appreciate the fundamental importance of the legal profession in the operation of social control. And from Professor Robert S. Lynd, I learned the urgent necessity of always attempting to relate technical sociological work to the complex problems confronting an industrial democratic society. The lessons taught by these two scholars were largely responsible for the conception of this research.

Finally, the patience and forebearance of Marion J. O'Gorman and Mark M. O'Gorman are gratefully acknowledged. Without their wise counsel and militant advocacy, this study would never have been completed.

H. J. O'GORMAN

New York
Christmas Day, 1962

CONTENTS

INTRODUCTION

CHAPTER 1

This monograph scrutinizes the matrimonial law practice of a group of lawyers in New York City. It is an analysis of the ways in which professional behavior is influenced by the structure of private practice, and as such, is a study of the sociology of professions. The data on which the report is based were gathered through interviews with eighty-two lawyers. The study has two major objectives: (1) To investigate some of the pressures impinging on a group of professionals who work in independent practice rather than in large formal organizations; and (2) to obtain some understanding of the part played by matrimonial cases * in contemporary law practice.

* A matrimonial case, in this study, refers to any type of legal problem handled by lawyers that alters, or is intended to alter, the legal status of a married couple. For the most part, these cases involve separation, divorce, and annulment actions.

Private Practice: The Non-bureaucratic Setting

In recent years, a number of studies have been done of professional role behavior in formal organizations. Although the specific topics have varied—professors in universities, psychiatrists in mental institutions, physicians in private and public hospitals, experts in labor unions, and so forth—the findings and analyses pertain uniformly, though not exclusively, to the performance of professional roles in bureaucratic organizations.[1] That this topic should attract scientific interest is easy to understand. The modern trends toward bureaucracy, the professionalization of many occupations, the increasing movement of professionals into more formally organized modes of group practice, and the potential conflict between the requirements of bureaucracy and the requirements of professional roles, make such a study a critical area for theoretical and applied sociology. Although this is an important line of research, its emphasis has led to a relative neglect of private professional practice.

If an adequate picture of the professions in modern society is to be achieved, professional work in private practice cannot be ignored. In fact, until more studies of private practice become available, inferences about the interplay of bureaucracies and professional roles must remain tentative. The exact nature of the impact of a bureaucracy on professional norms, values, attitudes, and skills, and of these characteristics on an organization, can be ascertained only through a comparative analysis of professional behavior in non-bureaucratic settings. For example, consider the issue of professional autonomy. It has been occasionally observed that professional independence is often jeopardized by the organizational demands of a bureaucracy; and it has been held, or implied, that this is not the case in private practice where, presumably, professionals have greater freedom.[2] This view overlooks the constraints that inhere in private practice. Involved as they inevitably are in patterned relationships with laymen and other professionals, private practitioners are subject to pressures that influence their behavior. As we shall see later, independent legal practitioners are not always free to exercise their professional judgments; more specifically, the kinds of cases they receive and the manner in which the cases are handled are influenced in large measure by characteristics of their law practices. Certainly, the constraining aspects of private practice are not limited to law. Thus, queries about the determinants of professional autonomy, and other questions about professional behavior, cannot be adequately answered until we have a clear understanding of prevailing work environments in and out of formal organizations.

Professional groups hold a position of acknowledged importance in contemporary society, and many of their members provide their services to the public through independent practice. An examination of the processes through which diverse types of practices are established and maintained would not only provide information about these occupational elites but also yield some understanding of precisely how available knowledge is applied to pressing human problems. Consequently, it is surprising that few attempts have been made to study the work-a-day world of private practitioners, to identify and analyze the variables that frustrate and facilitate the performance of professional skills in private practice.[3]

Perhaps one reason why this kind of work situation has not been systematically explored is that the pressures confronting private practitioners have a relatively low degree of visibility. The contrast with bureaucracies in this respect is quite marked. In hospitals, labor unions, corporations, universities, government agencies, and the like, organizational and professional role requirements are usually set forth quite explicitly. General rules, organizational charts, specific regulations, detailed record keeping, and group work involve highly visible phenomena. In private practice, on the other hand, such features, and their concomitant pressures, are less readily detected. Nevertheless, private practices can be classified by such attributes as organization of work, degree of specialization, types of clientele, and patterns of referral. In short, a private practitioner, like his bureaucratic colleague, works in a particular social and cultural environment that shapes and is shaped by his labor. It is, then, one of the goals of this study to examine some of the pressures affecting professional behavior in the non-bureaucratic milieu of private practice.

An investigation of matrimonial cases in private law practice is pertinent to this kind of inquiry. The general shift toward group practice notwithstanding, most American lawyers continue to practice alone; among those who work in groups, most practice with only one or two partners.[4] Generally speaking, legal practice is still free from direct bureaucratic constraints. However, if they regularly represent organizational clients, solo practitioners and partners in small firms may experience these constraints indirectly. Therefore, by concentrating our attention on matrimonial cases, where clients represent themselves as individuals and not organizations, we move the focus of our study still further away from the professional-in-bureaucracy model.[5]

Matrimonial Cases and Law Practice

The study of matrimonial practice presents much more than an occasion for looking at professional behavior in a non-bureaucratic setting. In its own right, this type of legal practice is an important and neglected area of research. It is important because the ways in which lawyers attempt to solve their clients' matrimonial problems affect the operation of the legal system. Whatever else law practice may involve, it consists of attorneys striving to handle the problems of laymen within the legal framework. For this reason, sociologists from Ross to Parsons have described the legal profession as a major mechanism of social control.[6] To understand this process of control, we need to describe and explain practitioners' efforts to deal with specific types of legal problems. As lawyers themselves have periodically observed, the influence of legal norms depends in no small way on the behavior of lawyers. And as Moore and Sussman noted some years ago: "An attempt to define the limits of the field of law and problems within it . . . must begin with the activities and ways of thinking of the practitioner." [7]

To suggest that the law can be understood, in part, by studying lawyers is not to advocate a naive form of legal realism. It is, rather, to emphasize the significance of the lawyer-client relationship for legal institutions. Laymen seek and act on the advice of counsel, and the variables that condition such advice are an important part of the total process of control. Consequently, the effects of matrimonial laws on those who would legally end their marriages depend partly on their lawyers' definitions of the problem. To discover the determinants of the latter's definitions requires, in turn, an investigation of matrimonial practice.

Aside from its implications for the legal system, a study of matrimonial practice should furnish some insight into contemporary law practice. In a society where hundreds of thousands of marriages are terminated annually, there are probably very few private practitioners who are not asked to represent a matrimonial client sometime during their careers. Because this kind of legal problem occurs frequently, an examination of its place in different types of law practices should illuminate some of the more general pressures that affect a lawyer's professional behavior.

Finally, a study of matrimonial cases provides an opportunity to discover some of the patterned ways in which attorneys receive, perceive, and deal with an important social problem. The comparative instability of American marriages has not escaped the serious attention of social scientists and lawyers. Psychologists and sociologists have produced a substantial body of research on the personal and social factors associated with marital instability.[8] Similarly, the legal consequences of the comparatively high rate of divorce in this country have generated a plethora of complex problems to which lawyers have addressed themselves.[9] Despite the great interest in the so-called divorce problem, the fact remains that no one has yet inquired into the professional participation of attorneys in the legal dissolution of their clients' marriages. To be sure, the lawyer's role in matrimonial actions has been discussed and debated, but the necessary empirical work has not been done.[10] Yet thirty years ago, a legal scholar and a social scientist commented on the significance of finding out what lawyers do with this type of case:

As divorce procedure is today organized, the lawyers play no insignificant part. . . . We ought to know a good deal more than is now known in any precise way concerning those persons who stand at the helm during the sinking of the matrimonial ship.[11]

The second major objective of this present study is to begin to fill this gap in knowledge with an analysis of the matrimonial practices prevailing among eighty-two attorneys.

Methodology

The data for this monograph were gathered through interviews with a sample of lawyers practicing in New York City.* The sample was selected in the following manner: (a) a list was compiled of all attorneys who represented matrimonial clients before the State Supreme Court in New York County during December 1957 and January 1958; [12] (b) from this list of 595 names, a 20 per cent random sample was drawn; (c) multiple name entries and names that could not be further identified through legal and telephone directories were eliminated from the sample. The final sample consisted of ninety-nine lawyers. From February to June, 1958, interviews were conducted with eighty-two of these attorneys. Among those who were not interviewed, six refused to participate, one died, and ten had work schedules that precluded anything but a superficial interview.

Each lawyer was initially reached by telephone; the purpose of the research was explained, and an appoint-

* The general characteristics of the sample are described in Appendix A. For related observations on problems encountered in interviewing lawyers, see the Methodological Note that appears as Appendix B.

ment made. All interviews were conducted by the writer in the informants' offices. With few exceptions, the informants expressed interest in the study and, without identifying specific clients or cases, cooperated fully in answering the questions.[13]

Plan of the Study

In order to render legal service, lawyers must know how to apply the law to their clients' problems. To do this they must take into account their clients' attitudes toward the law. In Chapter 2 we shall examine the legal norms and public attitudes concerning divorce to see what effects these two cultural items have on matrimonial practice in New York. Not all attorneys handle the same kinds of cases or represent the same kinds of clients. In Chapter 3 we discuss the variations in types of legal practices engaged in by our informants. Chapter 4 analyzes types of matrimonial practices. The diverse consequences of matrimonial cases for different kinds of practices are identified and related to a broader typology of private practice.

How do lawyers perceive and evaluate matrimonial actions? In what ways are these cases viewed as similar to, and different from, other types of legal problems? In Chapter 5, we attempt to answer these questions with an analysis of our informants' images of matrimonial cases. Chapter 6 presents lawyers' definitions of their professional role in marital cases. In it, the reported role definitions are correlated with the various orientations toward work and to types of practices.

The last chapter summarizes the major findings of the study and concludes by indicating several kinds of inquiry, each of which would enlarge our knowledge of professional behavior in the practice of law.

THE CULTURAL CONTEXT OF MATRIMONIAL PRACTICE

CHAPTER 2

The study of law practice inquires into a particular form of social behavior; it is an attempt to gather and analyze social facts. Two types of social facts can be distinguished: *cultural* facts referring to "transmitted and created content and pattern of values, ideas, and other symbolic-meaningful systems"; and *structural* facts designating "the specifically relational system of interaction among individuals and collectivities." [1] The distinction is analytical, not empirical, in that it differentiates two distinct ways of looking at the same phenomenon—one cannot be reduced to the other.

The distinction can be readily applied to professional practice. On the one hand, practice can be looked at with reference to such cultural facts as the content of professional knowledge, codes of ethics, and the sentiments of clients toward the profession. On the other hand, practice can be examined by searching for structural variables such as division of labor, organization of work, and patterns of interaction among professionals and between professionals and laymen.

In this chapter we are primarily concerned with some of the cultural components of law practice. More precisely, we shall delineate the cultural context of matrimonial practice in New York State. In the following two chapters we shift our analysis to some of the structural features of law practice in general and matrimonial practice in particular.

To practice a profession is to occupy a position between two cultures: the professional and the public. As professionals, practitioners share norms, values, attitudes, and knowledge with their fellow practitioners. But in order to serve laymen, professionals must also share prevailing public sentiments to some degree. Unless there is some consensus between professionals and laymen as to what problems require what kind of help, professional service cannot be rendered; unless practitioners are able to understand how laymen define and react to their problems, the application of professional skill and knowledge is limited. Professional practice, then, always occurs in a cultural context that is an amalgam of professional and public orientation toward designated problems.[2]

The cultural context of law practice is composed of two broad orientations. The professional orientation encompasses technical knowledge of the substantive and procedural elements of the legal system and an obligation to support that system. The public orientation consists of existing beliefs and attitudes concerning the law and its application to social life. To solve their clients' problems, lawyers must share both orientations. Although the orientations are different, the functioning of the legal system depends on the existence of some congruence between them. The absence of such congruence evokes a situation in which laws are ignored or evaded and in which lawyers find it difficult to represent clients without violating their own professional norms. We intend to show that precisely such an incongruity prevails in New York matrimonial law practice. The incongruity also characterizes the handling of matrimonial cases throughout the country, but, as we shall see, it takes a particularly acute form in New York State.

In order to analyze the cultural context of New York matrimonial practice, we must answer these questions: (1) What are the legal norms governing matrimonial dissolutions in New York? (2) How prevalent are divorce and other types of marital disruption in New York? (3) What are the public attitudes toward matrimonial dissolutions? (4) Are the New York laws being ignored or evaded? (5) What are the attitudes of the legal profession toward the state's matrimonial laws? (6) What dilemma, if any, does the cultural context pose for lawyers?

New York Matrimonial Laws

In New York a marriage can be legally terminated in four ways. First, it can be dissolved through an action for absolute divorce on only one ground—adultery. Second, a marriage can be concluded through an "Enoch Arden" decree, which can be granted upon proof that one of the spouses has been absent for five years and is presumed dead. Third, through annulment proceedings a marriage can be declared void when either of the parties: (a) is under eighteen years of age, (b) was incapable of consenting to the marriage for want of understanding, (c) was physically incapable of entering into the marital state, (d) consented to the marriage by reason of force, duress, or fraud, and (e) has been incurably insane for five years or more. Finally, a spouse may secure a judicial separation, that does not end the marriage but relieves the plaintiff of certain obligations of the relationship. When obtained by the wife, a separation usually enables her to receive support from her husband while relieving her of the obligation to live with him. When secured by the husband, a separation usually relieves him of the obligation to support his wife and provide a home for her. Four grounds for separation are available to either husband or wife: cruel and inhuman treatment, conduct of the defendant which renders it unsafe and improper for the plaintiff to live with the defendant, abandonment, and adultery. A fifth ground available to the wife is the neglect or refusal of the husband to provide for her.[3]

Perhaps the most significant characteristic of these laws is that, with one exception, they were enacted before the twentieth century. The divorce law dates back to 1787 when the state legislature first established divorce on the ground of adultery. In 1813 the remedy of separation was allowed but only for the wife. Annulment actions were authorized in 1830, and in 1880 separations became available to husbands. The "Enoch Arden" decree became law in 1922.

These legislative enactments reflect the traditional legal orientation toward dissolving the marriage contract. This orientation, which derives historically from canon law, rests on certain premises. It assumes that the state has an interest in protecting and preserving family life, and that the family is better protected if spouses are not free to terminate the marriage through mutual consent. It further assumes that only flagrant violations (defined by statute) of the marriage contract constitute proper grounds for dissolving or altering the marital relationship. It is also assumed that when marital norms are violated and a matrimonial action is initiated by the "injured" spouse, the defending spouse will appear in court to contest the action.

In general, New York matrimonial laws and the assumptions on which they rest are similar to the laws in other states.[4] There are, however, two important differences: New York is more conservative in recognizing grounds for divorce and more liberal in recognizing grounds for annulment. As noted above, there are no grounds for divorce in New York except adultery. All of the other states include, in addition to adultery, at least two other grounds. In fact, all but six states have five additional grounds.

New York's liberal annulment laws are primarily a result of judicial interpretation of the concept of fraud. In most states annulment actions based on fraud must pertain to what has been called the "essentials of marriage"; that is, the misrepresentations justifying an annulment "must affect the possibility of normal marital cohabitation." The application of this principle in case law has given it rather limited meaning: "concealed pregnancy by another man (at least in absence of premarital intercourse with plaintiff), and a concealed intent not to permit normal intercourse or maintain a normal home." [5] The New York Courts have taken a much broader view. They have held that the marriage contract may be voided on the same general basis as any other contract, and that the misrepresentations need not involve the "essentials" of marriage.[6]

Matrimonial laws are designed to control the conditions under which marriages are terminated. To understand more clearly the influence of New York laws on marital dissolutions, we need to examine the scope of marital disruption in the state.

Matrimonial Dissolutions in New York

During the past one hundred years there has been an increase in the number and rate of matrimonial dissolutions in this country. According to census records there were 120,996 divorced persons in 1890. In 1920 this figure had risen to 508,680, and in 1950 it was 2,444,245. The rate has risen in a similar fashion: in 1890 the rate of dissolution was .54 annually per 100 existing marriages; by 1920 it was up to 1.18 per 100; in 1950 it was 3.29.[7]

The pattern of matrimonial dissolution in New York State has generally followed the national trend. In 1890 the census listed 5,614 residents of the state as divorced. In 1920 the number was 23,735, and by 1950 it had reached 149,990. The correlative rate of divorce in the state was .24 per 100 married in 1890, .55 per 100 in 1920, and 2.00 per 100 in 1950.[8]

When the New York rates of recorded divorce are compared with those for the rest of the country, two facts emerge. First, the recorded rate in New York has been below the national average, and since 1950 the state has had the lowest divorce rate in the country. Although it has almost one-tenth of the nation's population, New York currently grants less than 2.5 per cent of the country's total dissolutions. Second, until recently the rate of recorded divorce in New York has increased more rapidly than the national rate. In the United States the number of divorced persons per 100 married was .54 in 1890 and 3.29 in 1950, representing an increase of 609 per cent. In New York the rate per 100 married was .24 in 1890 and 2.00 in 1950, an increase of 833 per cent. However, there is some indication that the state's rate may be declining. For example, from 1940 to 1948 there was an average of 9,600 divorce decrees granted each year; in 1956 there were about 4,750 divorces, the smallest in the State since 1932. Moreover, as a proportion of the state's total matrimonial dissolutions, divorces have decreased from 71 per cent in 1940 to 55 per cent in 1956.[9]

Aside from divorce, marriages may be terminated in New York through "Enoch Arden" decrees and annulments. The former do not substantially affect the state's total dissolution rate. They generally average about 560 per year, or less than one for every thirteen divorce decrees.[10]

Annulments, on the other hand, account for a remarkably large and growing proportion of the total dissolutions. Some idea of the significance of these actions in New York can be obtained by a comparison with the country as a whole. In 1946 there were about 22,000 marriages annulled in the United States; but even in that year, when the number of annulments was at its peak, they constituted only 3.5 per cent of all dissolutions. In New York annulments have represented about two-fifths of the state's total dissolutions during the past decade. During the 1950's, the state's average of 4,170 annulments per year was almost one-third of the total in the country.[11]

Within New York State, the largest concentration of matrimonial dissolutions occurs in New York City. In 1940 and 1950, for instance, the city's total dissolutions represented almost half of the state's total. In addition, the ratio of annulments to total dissolutions in New York City has followed the state pattern. In 1950, for example, 2,541 of the city's 5,644 dissolutions were annulments.[12]

The actual number and rate of dissolutions in New York State are difficult to ascertain because New Yorkers often establish temporary residences in other states to secure divorces. There are no adequate statistics on this pattern of migratory divorce. One careful estimate, made by Cahen on the basis of data for 1922, indicated that about 30 per cent of all divorces granted to New Yorkers were obtained outside the state.[13] More recently, Jacobson refers to statistics showing the place of birth for people remarrying in upstate New York that, in his opinion, "confirm Cahen's conclusion that a sizable proportion of New Yorkers secure divorces in other jurisdictions." [14] In the absence of adequate data, however, only one thing is sure: a substantial but unknown proportion of the state's residents terminate their marriages outside of New York.

Estimates of the total matrimonial disruption in New York must necessarily be speculative. Not only are data lacking for migratory divorces, but little is known of the numbers and rates of desertion. Even existing data present problems. The Census Bureau, for example, classifies as single those who report that their last marriage was annulled; and it includes in the category of married those who remarried after a previous divorce. Nevertheless, the present evidence seems to support Jacobson's conclusion: "Although the recorded divorce rate in New York is the lowest in the country, it is likely that annulments, migratory divorces, separations and desertions raise the total disruptions above the national level." [15]

Public Attitudes toward Divorce

It is frequently taken for granted that the increase in matrimonial dissolutions has been accompanied by a change in public attitudes toward divorce. Thus one writer observes that "radically changed attitudes" have transformed divorce from "a vaguely disreputable institution" to a "fashionable" one.[16] Another author writes of "the important shift in American attitudes toward marriage," a shift that "carried with it an experimental feeling toward marriage, with divorce seen no longer as a final disaster but as a temporary setback." [17] And a third observer notes that "the stigma attached to divorce has lessened, and public acceptance of remarriage has increased." [18] Such observations are indicative of a fairly widespread opinion that American attitudes toward matrimonial dissolutions have become more liberal than they were in the past. It is important to point out that this opinion has never been adequately documented. Consequently, we must at least identify some corroborating data.

The available evidence, although far from conclusive, tends to support the view that American attitudes have in fact become more liberal. Content analyses of interests and opinions in popular books and magazines indicate that divorce is more widely approved now than formerly.[19] A similar finding is reported in several studies of college students.[20] Public opinion polls show that younger people are more likely to have liberal attitudes toward divorce than older people.[21]

Books of etiquette also imply a change in attitude. For instance, in 1928 Emily Post reminded her readers that "conventions are shocked when divorced persons meet each other in apparent friendliness." In 1955, however, she records that "no rule of propriety has more completely changed than that which required all divorced people to meet as unspeaking strangers," and that "yesterday's ban against the bad taste of any approach of one [ex-spouse] to the other is gradually being lifted." [22]

Finally, the increasing rate of divorce can be interpreted as an index of a change in prevailing attitudes. This interpretation assumes, of course, a correlation between attitudes toward divorce and rates of divorce. Such a correlation is reported by Allardt for groups in Finland. He found that groups with liberal attitudes toward divorce had higher rates than those with conservative attitudes.[23] No similar research has been done in this country, but Goode's study includes data suggesting that the same relationship exists here. He reports that approval of divorce by parental families of spouses is greater in groups with a comparatively high divorce rate than it is among those with a lower rate.[24]

Although the evidence seems to suggest that public attitudes toward divorce have become more liberal, the legal norms controlling divorce have remained unchanged. The matrimonial laws in New York and throughout the country still mirror the traditional legal orientation; in every state matrimonial actions are still defined as legal controversies between "innocent" and "guilty" spouses. The fact that the legal norms have remained constant while public attitudes have apparently changed raises the important issue of public attitudes toward matrimonial laws. Data taken from four national opinion polls bear directly on the issue. In 1936 over three-fourths of a national sample answered "no" to the question, "Should divorces be easier to obtain in your state?" In 1937 a majority of another sample replied "no" when asked, "Do you think there should be easy divorce laws so that it would not be so expensive and troublesome to dissolve an unhappy marriage?" A third poll showed, in 1945, that less than 10 per cent expressed the opinion that their state divorce laws were "too strict"; in another poll conducted the same year, the majority did *not* favor recognition of Reno divorces by their states.[25] The data reported by these polls imply that most people accept their state divorce laws. A more recent poll might, of course, reveal a different picture. In fact, the earlier polls contain some hints that attitudes toward divorce laws were becoming more liberal. In three of the four studies cited, younger adults were more likely than older adults to: (a) favor "easy" divorce laws, (b) believe that their state laws were "too strict," and (c) favor recognition of Reno divorces. The data are, of course, only suggestive; age differences in attitudes are not equivalent to social change. To demonstrate such a shift in attitudes would require an examination of the impact of aging on attitudes within a specific generation, plus a comparison of an earlier generation's attitudes with those held by succeeding generations.

Although the divorce laws of all the states are similarly oriented, there is considerable variation in the number and content of grounds for divorce. It would therefore be instructive to analyze public attitudes toward divorce laws by states, but only one of the four polls provides the necessary data. In the 1936 survey, 77 per cent of a national sample were not in favor of easier divorce laws in their states. With one exception, this was the attitude of the majority in every state. The only deviant state was New York, where 51 per cent believed that it should be easier to secure a divorce in that state.[26] If we assume that attitudes toward divorce laws were more conservative in 1936 than they are today, this finding strongly suggests that there is a sharp discrepancy in New York between the legal theory of divorce and public attitudes. Furthermore, the fact that most people in other states were not in favor of "easier" divorce laws does not preclude the possibility that a similar discrepancy may exist throughout the country. For one thing, people may have one attitude toward divorce and a different attitude toward divorce law. More concretely, individuals may be favorably inclined toward the use of divorce as an expedient way of ending an unhappy marriage, yet simultaneously approve of existing matrimonial laws which make the attainment of divorce difficult. In addition, while public attitudes may be at odds with conservative legal norms, the administration of those norms may be sufficiently liberal to diminish, for all practical purposes, any discrepancy. In any event, more than attitude data are required to demonstrate the effects of an incongruity between legal and public orientations toward the dissolution of marriages; it must be shown that existing matrimonial laws are actually being ignored or evaded.

Institutionalized Evasion of Legal Norms

"The true problem is not to study how human life submits to rules—it simply does not; the real problem is how the rules become adapted to life." [27] Malinowski's comment certainly applies to the well-established system of evasion resulting from the adaptation of matrimonial laws, developed in ecclesiastical courts several centuries ago, to contemporary American life. That the laws are violated or evaded in most matrimonial actions today is generally acknowledged and repeatedly deplored.[28]

The evasion of matrimonial laws throughout the country is manifested in four patterns of behavior: [29] (1) The laws explicitly refuse to allow divorce through the mutual consent of the spouses, but most divorces appear to be based on mutual consent: (2) collusion between parties is prohibited, yet some degree of collusion is probably present in nearly every divorce action; (3) the law assumes that matrimonial actions will be contested, but most of them are not; (4) matrimonial actions are decided on the basis of evidence presented in court, but such evidence usually bears little relationship to the actual causes of marital disruption. In brief, every major premise underlying most matrimonial laws is persistently denied in the majority of matrimonial cases.

Norms, legal or otherwise, are not evaded without reason. When evasion becomes common practice among large numbers of law-abiding citizens, the determinants of such evasion are to be found, as Lincoln Steffens eventually realized, in institutional inconsistencies rather than in individual morality.[30] The extraordinary prevalence of evasion in matrimonial actions plainly points to a basic cultural conflict in which the legal norms governing the dissolution of marriage are incompatible with norms held by a large segment of American society. The laws prohibit what the public permits. Under these conditions patterns of evasive behavior have developed by which the law is obeyed in theory and denied in fact. To paraphrase Merton's analysis of political machines, the functional deficiencies of the law generate an alternative method to fulfill social demands somewhat more effectively.[31]

The evasion of matrimonial laws in New York is an extreme example of that found elsewhere. As in most other states, the majority of New York divorces are probably based on the mutual and collusive consent of the parties. Although direct evidence of this is not at hand, the extremely high proportion of undefended divorces makes it difficult to draw any other conclusion. It is estimated that about 90 per cent of the divorce actions throughout the country are not defended. A similar pattern prevails in New York. For example, from 1946 to 1950, in the New York boroughs of Bronx and Manhattan, 96 per cent of the divorces were uncontested.[32]

In addition to the absence of controversy, there are three other forms of evasion that appear to be more prevalent in New York than in other states. While migratory divorce, fraudulent cases, and the misuse of annulment laws undoubtedly occur in other jurisdictions, there is reason to believe that they take place with greater frequency in New York.

1. MIGRATORY DIVORCE Many New Yorkers, as observed earlier, establish temporary residences in other states to secure divorces. Although it is true that some people might prefer to end their marriages in some place other than their home communities, it is evident that the continual migration is primarily a reaction to New York's strict divorce law. In the words of one prominent attorney:

> While it may be true that some irresponsible spouses hie themselves to out-of-state divorce paradises to have a fling, it cannot be doubted that in the vast majority of cases the reason for the migration is the stringency of the divorce law in the home state. . . . The New York divorce law is an egregious example of the sort of unrealistic and uncompromising law that induces spouses to seek their freedom elsewhere.[33]

Since a migratory divorce is usually more expensive than one secured locally, this pattern of evasion is not equally open to all New Yorkers. If the state laws are easily avoided by financially independent residents, they can be avoided by others only at some sacrifice, and avoided not at all by those with low incomes. In this sense, the laws impinge differentially on the population; they are more binding on some groups than others. Contrary to popular belief, rates of divorce are higher for the working class than for the middle and upper classes.[34] Although those who are most likely to get divorced are least able to leave the state, they are apt to know, through the mass media, that divorce laws are frequently evaded by migratory divorces. The effect of this knowledge on their attitudes toward local divorce laws could readily motivate a functional equivalent of a migratory divorce: a fraudulent New York action.

2. FRAUDULENT NEW YORK CASES Periodic studies have revealed what many have privately believed: the vast majority of New York matrimonial cases involve illegal behavior. For example, the 1948 grand jury in New York County, after examining over 600 matrimonial actions and approximately 1,500 witnesses, turned in a presentment which included the following assessment:

> The investigation confirmed what had long been suspected: fraud, perjury, collusion and connivance pervade matrimonial actions of every type. In short, the Grand Jury is of the opinion that the present practices exude a stench and perpetuate a scandal involving the courts and the community.[35]

The grand jury discovered an entire deviant subculture that provided "a wholesale system of fabricating evidence for a divorce, the service of a correspondent and witness being supplied for a fee."[36] The immediate effects of the publication of the grand jury's findings attest to the scope of this deviant behavior. As soon as the findings were made known, hundreds of uncontested cases were adjourned at the request of counsel; and in New York County the number of matrimonial dissolutions decreased by two-fifths within a year.[37]

While the well-organized system of deviance may not have been replaced, the conditions that produced the system remain. Given the remarkable ease with which defendants are caught in "raids," the fact that the witnesses are invariably friends or relatives of the spouses, the dull similarity of the evidence offered, and the absence of contests, there is little reason to doubt those who believe that illegal behavior still characterizes most New York divorce cases. "The [Grand Jury] prosecutions may have destroyed the business [of manufactured cases]," writes Gellhorn, . . . "but the suspicion persists that many divorces are being obtained because of effective theatrical staging rather than because adultery was committed." [38]

3. DIVORCE THROUGH ANNULMENT The phrase, "divorce through annulment," is a legal contradiction—a marriage that is decreed to be nonexistent cannot be terminated. Socially speaking, the phrase refers to a procedure deliberately employed by many New Yorkers to terminate their marriages. The state's liberal annulment laws present an effective way to end a marriage for spouses who either cannot afford to leave New York or cannot or will not initiate a divorce action based on adultery. That annulment is widely used to circumvent New York divorce law is generally recognized.[39] There is no other plausible explanation for the disproportionately high number of annulments granted in New York. The state's average, it will be recalled, is almost one-third of the total annulments in the country.

The findings of even so brief an examination as this of the tactics used by spouses to evade matrimonial laws lend strong support to our contention that the legal and public orientations toward the dissolution of marriages are incongruous. We have yet to consider the attitudes of those who share both of these orientations—those who are sworn to uphold the laws that their clients so willingly evade.

Lawyers' Attitudes toward Matrimonial Laws

There is probably no part of the American legal system that has been subject to more detailed criticism by members of the legal profession than its matrimonial laws. This criticism, for the most part, has centered on the laws of divorce—laws that have elicited emotional, and often bitter, comment. Reginald Heber Smith gives this opinion: "In the whole administration of justice there is nothing that even remotely can compare in terms of rottenness with divorce proceedings." [40] A Maryland judge expresses a similar attitude toward divorce laws: "In the administration of those laws, fiction is heaped upon fiction, hypocrisy and cant are bolstered by subterfuge, men are forced either to do acts repugnant to their instincts of decency or to pretend that they have done such acts." [41] And yet another judgment concurs: "There is no area of law in which fact and fiction, reality and myth, truth and perjury, are so interwoven as in the operation of the present laws of divorce." [42] Essentially the same sentiments pervade most of the extensive legal literature dealing with matrimonial dissolutions. A review of this literature reveals substantial consensus among members of the bar on four points: matrimonial laws are not functioning adequately; illegal behavior pervades most matrimonial actions; illegal behavior is a result of a conflict between legal theory and public opinion; and a new legal approach to matrimonial problems is necessary. There is considerably less agreement, we might add, on what new legal approach should be attempted.

In New York the same type of professional criticism has been leveled at the state's matrimonial laws. In 1945 and again in 1950, the Association of the Bar of the City of New York drew public attention to what it described as the "sordid conditions which have surrounded actions for divorce, separation, and annulment of marriage in the State of New York"; and on both occasions the association recommended liberalizing the divorce law to "eliminate what has come to be recognized as a scandal, growing out of widespread fraud, perjury, collusion, and connivance which now pervade the dissolutions of marriages in this state." [43]

Evidence that these professional attitudes are representative of those held by attorneys who handle matrimonial cases in New York City was provided by the informants in our sample. When we asked them to express their views of the state's matrimonial laws, the answers they gave were:

They're terrible, just terrible. More grounds ought to be allowed. These people will seek a way out of the marriage anyway. One way or another, they are through with each other. They ought to be able to terminate their marriage here.

They stink, and please quote me. They ought to change the laws and make people honest. Why blacken the consciences of these people. We hate to go through this false adultery. The judges hate it. The odor of falseness is great.

The substantive law of divorce is hopelessly out of tune with the times. Second, the procedure is equally hopelessly out of tune. Third, as a result, people find evasive ways, unsound ways—and I disapprove—of dissolving their marriages. People didn't stop drinking during Prohibition; the law made no sense. So they find ways of evading it.

They are unrealistic. When a couple is hopelessly at odds with each other, there ought to be some way of dissolving the marriage without hurting someone. . . . So if a couple have money they get out of the state and get their divorce anyway. This way the poorer people are forced into these hotel-raid divorces.

No useful purpose can be served by adding further remarks in the same vein; they all have a striking similarity of content and tone. Only four of the eighty-two lawyers in the sample expressed the belief that New York matrimonial laws are adequate. All the rest were sharply critical.

Our informants' comments on the state's laws focused on three main objections: the laws are unrealistic, they discriminate against poor people, and they produce deviant behavior. We have already touched on these issues, but it will be helpful to examine in further detail how they appear to practicing attorneys.

1. Unreal Law   About one of every four informants criticized New York matrimonial laws as being unrealistic. "It's ridiculous," commented one attorney, "there's a certain ritual which everyone follows. It has no connection with reality at all." According to these informants, the laws fail to be realistic in two important respects. First, the laws in no way interfere with divorce through mutual consent. "People who want a divorce," said a lawyer, "get it one way or another. The law as it exists certainly doesn't stop anyone." Second, the legal norms run counter to present public attitudes that accept the dissolution of unhappy marriages through the mutual consent of the spouses. And, as the next set of excerpts implies, these attorneys tend to be sympathetic toward couples who decide to end their relationship:

I feel that marriage is a good thing and you should make it stick. But people should not be made to stick together.

Why should people have to live together when they are unhappy? It doesn't make sense.

In my opinion, every person has the right to do what he wants with reference to a marriage provided the children are protected.

2. ECONOMIC DISCRIMINATION One of five informants objected to the New York divorce law because it discriminates against the poor. "My main gripe," an informant told us, "is that it works only for the rich, or at least in their favor." What he had in mind, of course, was the extent to which the financial resources of matrimonial clients influence their ability to secure a migratory divorce. As we were repeatedly reminded, "The rich leave the state." That the solution to a client's legal problem is affected by his economic status is certainly not restricted to matrimonial cases. Nevertheless, it constitutes, in the eyes of many lawyers, a serious indictment of the state's divorce law.

3. GENERATING DEVIANT BEHAVIOR Slightly more than two out of five lawyers criticized state law because, in their opinion, it produced perjury, collusion, subornation, and connivance. This critique was made in sociological terms, for they see the illegal behavior, to use Plant's incisive description, as "the normal behavior of normal people in an abnormal situation." [44] Or as one attorney expressed it: "The law as it now stands encourages people to lie, to commit perjury." After describing the various matrimonial laws as "inhuman" and "stupid," another lawyer added: "They generate perjury, deceit, and lying."

In linking this deviance to institutional sources, the informants were stating several significant ideas. First, as was just pointed out, they hold the structure of the law accountable for deviant behavior which they understand as a reaction to laws "hopelessly out of tune with the times." Correlatively, they were convinced that a change in law would eliminate the undesirable behavior.

Second, they implicitly confirmed, on the basis of their experience, that evasion of the law is characteristic of most New York matrimonial cases. One informant gave this estimate of the prevalence of evasion: "You could throw a dart blindly and say, 'this one is phony,' and you'd be right most of the time."

Third and most significant is the idea that the evasion is a matter of common knowledge among lawyers and judges. "The amount of perjury is terrible," admitted an attorney, "I know it; the judges know it; we all know it." This idea exemplifies a significant variation of the general pattern known as pluralistic ignorance, the pattern in which individual group members *mistakenly* believe that their own attitudes are at odds with or similar to those held by others in the group. In this particular instance, the pattern takes a special form: Members of the legal profession *privately* recognize that they in fact share the knowledge that matrimonial laws are consistently broken; but this private knowledge is accompanied by institutional silence, for the courts proceed on the empirically unwarranted assumption that matrimonial cases are legally valid.[45] The knowledge that the evasion is known to and permitted by the courts is especially important; it is interpreted by many lawyers to constitute judicial acceptance of illegal behavior. Thus, an informant concluded his description of collusion in these cases by saying: "It is done with the consent of the judges."

The fact that the evasion of law is known to officers of

the court symbolically legitimatizes the behavior; it is given tacit institutional approval. No matter how much each lawyer or judge personally dislikes what he is a party to, the general absence of punitive action structurally stamps the evasion as acceptable. However, this legitimation of evasion exists only when two conditions are clearly present: (a) While many matrimonial cases may in fact be collusive or based on perjury, they at least meet all the technical requirements of the law; (b) lawyers and judges undoubtedly recognize that by allowing the evasion to persist, the law is being used to break the law in order to serve an important social function. "Men of most renowned vertu," wrote Milton, "have sometimes by transgressing, most truly kept the law." [46]

The Lawyers' Dilemma

Attorneys who participate in matrimonial cases are faced with a dilemma: while they are obligated to uphold laws whose deficiencies they acknowledge and lament, they represent clients whose problems they are expected to solve without violating laws or professional ethics. The problem is further complicated because, although evasion of matrimonial laws is accepted tacitly, it is still illegal and officially proscribed by the profession. In these cases, therefore, lawyers are commonly described as being in "an equivocal and uncomfortable position." [47] This problem exists to some extent in most types of legal cases, but, on the basis of our discussion so far, it would seem particularly characteristic of matrimonial cases. It is difficult to disagree with Ploscowe's judgment: "No branch of the law throws more of a strain upon a lawyer's conscience or tends as much to befuddle the Canons of Ethics as the practice of divorce law." [48]

The professional dilemma just described can be seen more clearly in sociological terms.[49] To be a lawyer is to occupy a specific social status or position. An occupant of this status is related to a number of role partners: clients, law partners, opposing counsel, bar associations, judges, and witnesses. These role relationships which an individual has because he holds this particular status constitute his role-set. For a lawyer to discharge his professional obligations there must be some degree of order prevailing in his role-set; there must be some minimum consensus of mutual normative orientations stabilizing the role relationships. This stability is threatened whenever role partners have normative expectations that differ from those held by the status occupant. It is also threatened when role partners hold incompatible or conflicting expectations, a situation that frequently exists when a lawyer represents a matrimonial client. Members of the bar and bench officially expect that a lawyer will uphold matrimonial laws; clients, on the other hand, expect a lawyer to help them terminate their marriages. Since this disturbance in the role-set derives from the broader incongruity between legal and public cultures, it manifests, at the interpersonal level, the cultural context of matrimonial practice in this country.

The lawyers' dilemma in handling these cases involves a professional role conflict: lawyers are exposed "to conflicting sets of legitimized role expectations such that the complete fulfillment of both is realistically impossible." [50] Attorneys may attempt to cope with this conflict in one of three ways. They can, of course, avoid matrimonial cases completely. If the cases are accepted, the conflict can be reduced by conformity to one of the two conflicting expectations. A lawyer may insist, for example, on strict adherence to legal requirements and refuse to accept a case in which such adherence is not possible:

I, myself, refuse to touch a divorce case in New York where the evidence is not absolutely unimpeachable. For instance, where there is a case of open and flagrant adultery. But in any case where there is some doubt about the evidence, I won't take it at all.

Or a lawyer may give priority to the client's expectations and deliberately evade the law:

Many lawyers, including myself, send [matrimonial clients] out of the state simply to avoid the adultery issue.

I know where possible we resort to annulment proceedings rather than go through that adultery routine.

However the role conflict may be handled, it is a source of frustration for those who practice matrimonial law. Evidence of this frustration among our informants can be illustrated in three ways. The question asking for an informant's opinion of New York matrimonial laws evoked, in many instances, highly affective reactions. Typically, lawyers would reply to our opening queries in a polite and cautious manner. As the interview progressed, the informants usually became less restrained and frankly discussed various aspects of law practice. Although many of them appeared to be deeply interested in the study, they generally kept their professional demeanor; their answers were expressed, for the most part, in a thoroughly detached way. However, when we requested their views of New York laws, many reacted in a much less impersonal manner. Some got up from their desks and walked around the office while replying.

One attorney went to his office door, called in his partner, and with a snort, asked to have the question repeated. When this was done, both of them laughed. In addition, several lawyers requested that they not be quoted on the question, and others wanted assurance that they would be quoted. This particular question was the only one in the interview to evoke such marked behavioral changes.

This same question often elicited a distinct shift in the ways in which informants expressed themselves. Aside from the content of their answers, the perjorative nature of the phrases used suggests that the words were carrying much more than the manifest freight of legal criticism. Here is a sample of terms used by lawyers to describe the matrimonial laws of New York: "farce," "ridiculous," "stink," "terrible," "incredible," "asinine," "cockeyed," "stupid," "horror," "inhuman," "fantastic," "outrageous," and "puritanical." The repeated use of these and similar epithets in an otherwise calm interview may be interpreted provisionally to indicate (a) that the query tapped feelings of tension related to role conflict, and (b) that some of the tension was released through the use of highly affective language.

A final and more direct piece of evidence of professional frustration is found in the replies to the question bearing on the controversial aspects of the matrimonial laws of New York State. These answers often included direct references to lawyers' personal feelings. Sometimes these feelings were expressed as the informants talked of their participation in undefended cases:

> Ninety per cent of the undefended matrimonials are based on perjury. They are all arranged. The raids are made with the consent of the defendant. We all know this. The judges know it. *It's embarrassing to go* [*to court*].

[The laws] are a farce. . . . I have in mind especially the undefended matters before official referees. You have these black nightgown routines with the man in the blue shorts. *I tell you it's insulting to a lawyer.*

In other interviews the frustration was verbalized when attorneys discussed the problem of dealing with clients who have no grounds for a matrimonial action in New York:

These laws make my life tougher. I'm put in a position where I'm dealing with people who can't or won't be reconciled. In a layman's sense, they feel that they have grounds but legally they haven't, and there's nothing I can do for them.

I have a case now where the husband refuses to allow the wife to get a divorce in another jurisdiction. . . . Grounds of cruelty and nonsupport clearly exist . . . they should be divorced. In another state they would. *This kind of thing is very trying on a lawyer.*

Even where matrimonial clients are able to leave New York to secure their divorces, their lawyers may remain at home feeling ambivalent about this exercise of their professional role. More than a few members of the New York Bar would probably agree with the following evaluation of the lawyers' dilemma:

The legal profession is caught: either they help their clients in a New York action where we have to act like blind monkeys, or we help them engage in the sophistry of an out-of-state divorce in Mexico or Alabama. Why they don't even give up their apartments or jobs as they establish residence in another state. *I know they're coming back. I feel very sensitive about it, but I don't know what else to do.*

In this chapter we have examined some cultural variables that influence the practice of matrimonial law, variables that produce not only institutionalized evasion of legal norms but also a professional role conflict among members of the legal profession. This is, of course, only part of the picture. Culture does not directly shape social behavior; its effects are altered by intermediate structural variables. If we are to trace the impact of these cultural variables on social behavior and to identify some of the relevant structural variables affecting that impact, we need to look at the social context of law practice.

THE SOCIAL CONTEXT OF LEGAL PRACTICE:

Types of Law Practice

CHAPTER 3

The cultural context of matrimonial practice in New York does not affect all lawyers equally. Since lawyers engage in different kinds of matrimonial practice, there is considerable variation in their actual experience with the problems that attend the conflict between public opinion and legal norms over the requirements for divorce. The differences in matrimonial practice, however, are largely the result of differences in types of law practices. In this chapter we describe the characteristics of our informants' legal practices, and in the next chapter we discuss the related patterns of their matrimonial work.

Urban Law Practice

The urbanization of Western life has altered the character of professional work. For most of the professions the pattern of change has been the same: an increasing concentration of practitioners in large cities, greater specialization of work, and a pronounced tendency toward group practice. Because alterations in the nature of work inevitably raise problems of recruitment, training, and control, these changes have elicited considerable discussion among professionals.[1] Certainly, in law, an attorney who practices in a city like New York faces working conditions not found in smaller communities of the past or present. Since the types of law practices prevailing among our informants represent various modes of adjustment to metropolitan conditions, we need to examine some of the characteristics of urban law practice.

The contemporary American bar is highly urbanized. In 1958, of the slightly more than 262,000 lawyers in the nation, 53 per cent worked in cities with populations of 200,000 or more, while 39 per cent of the total were located in cities with a half a million or more inhabitants. The greatest concentration is in New York City where more than 30,000 attorneys, about 12 per cent of the national total, practice law. In contrast, the proportion of lawyers in smaller cities and towns has declined steadily over the past two decades.[2] Although the concepts of supply and demand do not describe accurately the market for professional services, it is evident that the distribution of attorneys partly reflects the large urban demand for legal services.

The urban demand for services is as diverse as it is large. The growth of legal specialization, a marked characteristic of modern practice, is partly a response to the increased diversity of demand. There is no way of knowing with any degree of accuracy how many legal specialties currently exist, nor what proportion of lawyers are specialists. However, the data collected by Kent, in his study of the Chicago bar, probably roughly describe the situation in most large cities. He found that 55 per cent of a sample of 810 attorneys reported some degree of specialization, and that most of the specialization reported occurred in ten fields.[3] Additional, though more indirect, evidence of the scope of present specialization may be seen in the wide variety of bar association committees. In 1950, for example, the New York County Lawyers Association had the following standing committees: Admiralty; Aeronautical Law; Arbitration and Conciliation; Banking and Insurance; Bankruptcy; Communications; Foreign Law; International Law; Labor Relations; Patents, Trademarks and Copyrights; Real Property; Securities and Exchange; and Taxation. The same bar association also had special committees on problems in administrative law, military justice, socio-legal jurisprudence, and workmen's compensation.[4]

Specialization and urbanization are closely associated. Large cities present markets for which, in small towns and rural areas, there is little demand. A lawyer who specialized in criminal or patent law would have difficulty in maintaining his practice in a small town, because the incidence of such cases is apt to be low. A large city, on the other hand, will have enough such cases to support a number of specialists. Hence, the efflorescence of legal specialties has been confined mainly to the bar in metropolitan areas.

Changes in the law itself have also fostered specialization. The last sixty years have witnessed the emergence of entirely new fields of practice in such areas as administration, workmen's compensation, labor, and taxation. At the same time, the more traditional fields have become increasingly complicated by a constant proliferation of statutes and judicial decisions at the federal, state, and local levels. Indeed, the law has become so complex that specialization is often the only way lawyers can maintain their competence.[5]

An increase in the division of labor normally is accompanied by alterations in the organization of work. Accordingly, the trend toward legal specialization has been paralleled by a shift toward group practice. Although most attorneys throughout the country still practice alone, the tendency in recent years is in the direction of more group practice. Thus, in 1947, three-fourths of the nation's independent lawyers were solo practitioners; seven years later, in 1954, the proportion of individual practitioners had dropped to slightly under two-thirds.[6]

The most publicized form of group practice is done in large law firms located in metropolitan centers. Many of the organizational attributes of these so-called "law factories," attributes like intensive specialization, the team handling of problems, a greater reliance on office counseling rather than courtroom advocacy, and the recruitment of a relatively restricted type of clientele, represent a sharp departure from the traditional picture of law work as practiced by the independent attorney.[7] These attributes, however, are not confined to "law factories"; to a lesser extent, they aptly portray the structure of many small and medium-size firms.[8] Furthermore, these same features are clearly discernible in the organization of urban legal aid societies.[9] To the degree that the trend toward group practice continues, these structural characteristics of work, so clearly delineated in the largest firms, will increasingly shape the practice of law.

The movement into specialized work and group practice is reinforced by economic motivations. As a rule, general practitioners receive lower incomes than specialists, and the incomes of solo practitioners are considerably less than those received by firm partners. The differences in incomes are not insignificant: lawyers in firms consisting of between five and eight members receive on the average over three times as much income as those in individual practice; and in firms with nine or more partners, the earnings of each are almost five times those received by solo practitioners.[10] This pattern of differential incomes gives lawyers, particularly those in large cities, a strong incentive to specialize and practice in firms.

Two other facts about legal incomes are relevant. First, there is a fairly consistent relationship between the size of a community in which a lawyer works and his annual income. The highest average incomes are received by attorneys in the largest metropolitan areas. Second, although the average income increases with community size, the spread of incomes around the mean value also increases. Consequently, the greatest range of incomes is found among lawyers in the largest cities; moreover, it varies most among solo practitioners. The dispersion of incomes has always been greater in law than in other professions. But while this dispersion has lessened in the last decade, law practice in big cities still produces a greater proportion of extreme incomes than is found in smaller population centers.[11] At least two conditions account for this situation. On the one hand, as we noted earlier, a disproportionately large number of lawyers is concentrated in large urban areas. On the other hand, the most financially rewarding legal business is monopolized by a comparatively small number of attorneys in large firms. Under such circumstances, the majority of urban practitioners must compete with each other for the relatively less lucrative sources of legal work.[12]

Competition is, of course, a major characteristic of the legal profession and an outstanding feature of urban practice. In diverse ways, it affects the experiences of law students, young lawyers, and established practitioners alike.[13] Competition in law practice takes two forms. First, the legal profession competes with other professions and occupations in rendering legal service to the public. From the profession's point of view, this involves a collective battle against the unauthorized practice of law, a battle in which bar associations have been extremely militant if not always successful.[14] Second, lawyers compete among themselves for clients. This form of competition bears more directly on this discussion, and it usually has been discussed, debated, and defined by the profession within the limited vocabulary of supply and income. This was particularly true during the last depression when it was common to infer that the bar was "overcrowded" by simply relating the size of legal incomes to the number of lawyers per population.[15] Given the steady rise of legal incomes in postwar years, the recent decline in the number of entrants to the profession,[16] and the recognition of the fallacious reasoning involved, this type of formulation soon lost much of its significance. It is important to note, however, that this kind of formulation diverted attention from other significant variables in the competitive process. Specifically, it ignores the fact that a professional's competitive position tends to depend more closely on personal and social characteristics than upon strictly technical qualifications. Competition does not occur uniformly throughout the bar in any given community; each lawyer is not, except in an abstract sense, competing with all other lawyers. Rather, the competition takes place within submarkets that are defined primarily, though not entirely, by nonprofessional statuses such as age, sex, religion, ethnic background, and class origins. In short, the competition is highly imperfect. Except when used as indices of technical competence (as in the use of the term "young" to connote inexperience) these statuses constitute latent social identities.[17] That is, they are not culturally prescribed as relevant to the practice of law. Prescribed or not, a lawyer's ability to compete is affected by his latent identities.

The effects of latent attributes on law practice actually begin to appear before attorneys start to practice, in fact even before they enter professional school. Although once in law school, students compete in their ability to master technical knowledge, their admission to various kinds of schools is affected to a considerable degree by their economic, religious, and ethnic attributes. Available evidence indicates that law schools of major universities recruit a greater proportion of students who are of Anglo-Saxon, Protestant, and high socioeconomic background, than do Catholic and independent law schools.[18] This variation in recruitment is significant because the type of law school attended governs the kind of practice first engaged in by young lawyers. For example, a recent study showed that graduates of university-affiliated schools were more apt to be employed by firms than were graduates of independent or Catholic institutions; and graduates of independent schools were more likely than other graduates to establish their own practice or to take jobs outside of law.[19]

The relationship between law school and initial employment is not due simply to a selective process of recruitment; the relationship depends also on discriminatory hiring practices prevailing in the profession. Many law firms have a policy of not hiring Negro, Jewish, or women lawyers. Furthermore, the importance of such extraprofessional attributes as determining variables in the hiring practices of law firms is supported by the reluctance of most law firms to admit publicly that they have openings; in fact, they sometimes go to great lengths to hide their personnel needs. Although this practice makes it more difficult for applicants to locate jobs, it allows employers greater freedom to choose among applicants on other than technical qualifications.[20]

Latent identities continue to affect law practice well beyond the period of early employment, as the following set of otherwise disparate findings illustrate: Lawyers who graduated from Harvard and Yale Law Schools are less likely to establish solo practices than graduates of other schools; compared to most other lawyers, Jewish attorneys are more apt to practice alone or in predominantly Jewish firms; except in rare instances, all women members of the bar are salaried employees; almost all Negro practitioners rely on exclusively Negro clienteles; about one-third of the partners in twenty large New York City law firms are listed, or belong to families who are listed, in the Social Register.[21] Similarly, the professional experiences of men like Simeon Eben Baldwin and George Wharton Pepper, or Fiorello La Guardia and Louis Waldman, as well as many others, plainly reveal that in law, as elsewhere, the ability to compete depends on something more than technical proficiency in a field of work.[22]

The inability of laymen to judge the competency of professional services further contributes to the importance of lawyers' nontechnical attributes. This is probably less true in law and accounting than in medicine or dentistry, and, within law, probably less true of business clients than others. Nevertheless, an attorney's aptitude for attracting and retaining clients is conditioned, as how-to-do-it manuals often point out, by his "personality" and "personal contacts." [23]

The relevancy of nonprofessional characteristics is also strengthened by the anonymity of urban life. The sheer size and density of urban populations, often subdivided into a myriad of heterogeneous communities and neighborhoods, make the problem of client-recruitment more difficult than in smaller towns. The problem is compounded by ethical prohibitions against advertising, a professional ideology proclaiming all attorneys equally competent to practice, and the presence of a large supply of practitioners. Under these conditions, as Llewellyn once observed, "It is impossible for anybody but half a dozen or half a hundred firms to have their names spoken around from mouth to mouth so that people know who they are, what they can do, and what they charge." [24] To solve the problem of anonymity a lawyer needs to know not law, but people, for before he is given work as a professional, he must first be known in some other status. Joining ethnic, religious, social, fraternal, and political organizations is, of course, a familiar way of becoming known. But since organizational membership, whether in formal or informal groups, is built on shared values, an attorney is most likely to become known among those with whom he already shares certain personal and group identities. Thus, in a large city, with its attending anonymity, a lawyer is especially dependent on the network of communications that he can establish through statuses technically irrelevant to the exercise of his professional skills.

The effect of nonprofessional characteristics is not unrelated to the more technically relevant variables. Evidence of legal ability—as reflected, for example, in law school grades[25] or in the publicized handling of cases —alters an attorney's competitive position. In like manner, variations in the demand for legal talent influence the comparative significance given to either professional or nonprofessional attributes. In general, as demand increases, the emphasis on technical competence increases, and the weight assigned to personal and social characteristics, though never eliminated, tends to lessen.[26]

This discussion of specialization, group practice, and competition barely begins to describe the complexities of contemporary law practice. It outlines, however, what appear to be the major aspects of urban practice. With this brief introduction, we are ready to examine the types of legal practice prevailing among our informants.

Types of Law Practice

Three types of law practice were identified: general, concentrated, and specialized. The major criterion for distinguishing these types was found in the diversity of legal work reported by each lawyer. A general practice is one in which a comparative variety of legal problems are usually encountered. Specifically, a practice was classified as *general* if an informant said that he handled normally four or more types of legal problems, no one of which dominated his work. A practice in which a lawyer deals primarily but not exclusively with a narrow range of legal problems may be called *concentrated* or semi-specialized. Practices were classified as concentrated if an attorney stated that, while most of his work focused on one or two types of cases, he also dealt consistently, but to a lesser degree, with other types of legal problems. *Specialized* practices have the least amount of diversity, and a practice was so classified if a lawyer indicated that his work was restricted generally to one or two kinds of cases.

Of the eighty-two lawyers in our sample, twenty-nine were assessed on the basis of their work descriptions as being in general practice, forty-one in concentrated practice, and twelve in specialized practice. Expressed in percentages, 35 per cent of the informants were general practitioners, 50 per cent were semi-specialists, and 15 per cent were fully specialized. These types differ from one another by: (1) organization of practice, (2) length of time in practice, (3) lawyers' class background, (4) clients' class background, (5) types of cases handled, and (6) types of matrimonial practice. In the following sections we shall discuss the first five of these differences and then turn our attention, in the next chapter, to the varying patterns of matrimonial practice.

Organization of Practice

Although the recent trend has been toward group practice, most lawyers, as noted previously, still practice alone. Among our informants, forty-eight were solo practitioners. The remaining thirty-four practiced with others in the following statuses: three were salaried associates; sixteen were partners in two-partner firms; ten were partners in three-partner firms; and five were partners in firms with four or more partners.

Organization of work and type of practice are mutually dependent: specialists tend to practice in groups more than general practitioners, and group practice is performed most efficiently through a division of labor. The more our informants' practices were specialized, the more they were apt to be practicing as partners. The proportion of lawyers in partnerships rises from 30 per cent among general practitioners, to 43 per cent of those in concentrated practices, and to 50 per cent of those in fully specialized work. Correlatively, 40 per cent of the solo practitioners but only 26 per cent of those in partnerships were in general practice.

For several reasons, the relationship between organization and type of practice is subject to some variation. First, general practitioners may enter partnerships without any appreciable decline in the diversity of work handled by each partner. However, the partners to such an arrangement may have to assume responsibility for different phases of their practice. In other words, though the work remains general for all, one may be assigned the task of running the office, another for trying cases in court, and perhaps another for recruiting clients. That some such division of work inheres in even the most general forms of practice is reflected in the following complaints of two solo general practitioners:

> My biggest mistake was remaining by myself. . . . Going it alone is too tough. You can't be in the office and circulating at the same time. And you have to circulate to get known. But then office work takes a lot of time, a great deal of clerical work. It's very hard for one man to do all of that.

> A lawyer to live must have volume. I have volume but it is killing me. I'm in court all day almost every day in the week. When I get back to the office . . . there are phone calls, messages, I have to give dictation, consult with other lawyers. I'm so busy I lose business. . . . Ideally, you should have three lawyers: an office man, a court man, and a man going back and forth between the two.

Second, admission to group practice is controlled by group norms, and a lawyer's latent identities may well determine with whom he can and cannot practice. For example, though religious discrimination in the hiring of attorneys is believed to be declining, the evidence suggests that most Jewish lawyers are still forced to practice with each other or alone. Thus, the data in hand reveal that seven out of ten of our Jewish informants in group practice worked in Jewish firms.[27] In a similar fashion, the organization of a Negro's legal practice is influenced by the social consequences attending his racial status. Excluded from white firms, and dependent on the nonwhite community for clients, nearly all Negro lawyers must practice alone or with each other. Given the comparatively low demand for their services, as well as their general interest in being independent, most Negro attorneys, like the six out of seven in our sample, probably will be found practicing alone.[28]

Finally, the relationship between specialization and group practice should not be exaggerated. It is not specialization per se that moves lawyers into firms, but specific types of specialization. If it is evident that the many legal problems of large corporate clients can be handled only by a team of legal specialists, it is equally clear that no such organization is required for specialization in matrimonial, criminal, personal injury, probate, collection, immigration, and other kinds of cases.[29]

Length of Time in Practice

A lawyer's type of practice is also related to the length of time he has been practicing. In general, the longer he practices, the more likely he is to concentrate or specialize. The median number of years in practice for all lawyers in our sample was 23. The median for general practitioners was 13; for those in concentrated practice it was 25; and among the specialists it was 29.

The association between years in practice and specialization is not unexpected. Beginners rarely possess either the skill or opportunity to perform specialized work. However, this finding does suggest that in law, as in medicine, careers may entail a steady movement away from general practice.[30] This is not to imply that lawyers, as they gain experience, begin to specialize deliberately; on the contrary, most specialized legal practices are largely unplanned responses to the exigencies of a particular law practice.

Most lawyers, when they first attempt to establish a practice, are probably required to be general practitioners. This is particularly true of young attorneys who labor under the twin handicaps of anonymity and inexperience; consequently, they must be willing to take any kind of case. For them, necessity is the mother of diversity. Moreover, the cases they receive during this period are apt to be as minor as they are diverse. "Most young lawyers," observed an elderly informant, "have to struggle along doing a lot of little things for people." At this stage, much of an attorney's time may be taken up with "small stuff": comparatively inconsequential cases handled for little or no fees. This "small stuff"—tenant complaints against landlords, traffic violations, debt collections, minor criminal offenses, and so forth—is accepted partly out of need and partly in anticipation of future work. A young lawyer explained why he kept taking otherwise futile collection cases:

> There's no satisfaction in collecting debts. But every lawyer has to start out doing it. Most of the time it is impossible to collect. . . . But you have to show that you can do a job and hope that some legal work will come your way.

In a similar vein, another young informant pointed to the potential effect of accepting cases for low fees:

Where you don't get much money, you got to figure that the client may refer some business to you in the future.

During this so-called "starvation period," lawyers are inclined to do more than hope and wait passively for cases. To lessen their professional anonymity and to recruit clients, they attempt to become known to as many people as possible. This campaign for clients implies, of course, a willingness to accept any kind of legal problem. An eminently successful attorney with a concentrated real estate practice had this to say about his early days at the bar:

How does a young man build up clients? He has to get out and sell himself. I did. I went to all sorts of social events, to parties, to bars and saloons in order to get known. I must have given out over a thousand cards with my name on them. . . . In those days I took whatever I could get.

A willingness to accept all types of cases does not mean that all types will be available. For, as we shall shortly indicate, general practice, whether engaged in by young or older lawyers, is confined to designated kinds of cases. More importantly, although the work of young practitioners covers an appreciable range of marginal legal problems, a significant pattern of similar cases often appears within that range. In some instances, the pattern does not persist, and practice remains diversified. But, and this is the important point, if such a pattern persists, it often forms the nucleus of a concentrated or specialized practice.

The emergence of a sequence of similar cases is significant because law schools do not prepare attorneys for practice in specific fields of law.[31] As a result, early professional experience tends to define the areas in which lawyers become competent, and, concomitantly, it makes available selected sources of further work. A pattern of similar cases hastens the acquisition of practical skill and knowledge within particular legal fields and increases interaction with lawyers and clients with problems in those fields. This relatively early differential exposure to legal work operates, therefore, to move many lawyers away from general practice and into some type and degree of specialization. And this process, as the next excerpt states, occurs independently of lawyers' personal inclinations:

A lawyer's work is determined by what kind of clients he gets in the beginning. If you start out with a certain type of case, you get more and more of the same thing. You may not like the type, but you are forced to handle it.

This process of specialization through differentiated experience may be accelerated by two events. First, the appearance of a "regular" client, one who retains an attorney on an annual basis, usually focuses counsel's attention on legal fields relevant to that client's problems; it also increases the probability that similar clients will be referred. Second, specialization is frequently the product of a "big" case, a case that receives widespread publicity in the professional journals or the public press. The publicity attending such cases often brings to the participating lawyers a succession of similar cases which frequently alters the character of their practice.[32] For example, one informant traced the origins of his highly specialized practice back to the impact of one "big" case. Since his comments provide a compact summary of our discussion, we quote him at length:

It all came about because of one case. You know a lawyer, unless someone sets him up in practice, has a tough time. You have to rely on friends and associates as a young man to bring you matters. . . . It's very tough. . . . Depending on the kinds of cases they get as young men, lawyers may become specialists in one thing or another. For many, a lot depends on that one, or two, early and big cases, the case that brings them to the attention of other people or other lawyers. That's what happened to me, my lucky break. A friend sent me this case of a minority stockholder's suit against the X Company. . . . I studied it carefully . . . and advised that they proceed with the suit. Well, we went ahead and fought for several years and finally won a million-dollar suit. Immediately, other lawyers started bringing me similar cases, and I have been in this specialty ever since.

The effect of time in practice on degree of specialization is qualified by other variables; not all general practitioners become specialists, and a small proportion of lawyers begin their careers in specialized fields of work.[33] A more complete analysis of all the variables influencing the process of legal specialization is outside the purview of this discussion. However, it is instructive to note that the relationship under review is affected indirectly, as reported in the next section, by the lawyer's class background.

Lawyers' Class Background

For three-fourths of the lawyers in our sample, admission to the legal profession was a move upward from their fathers' position in the occupational hierarchy: 23 per cent of these attorneys had fathers who earned their living as skilled or unskilled laborers; 11 per cent of them had fathers who held such white collar jobs as office workers, salesmen, and school teachers; 42 per cent had fathers who owned or managed small business enterprises such as grocery stores, jewelry shops, restaurants, and tailor shops; finally, 24 per cent had fathers who were business executives or professionals, of whom only five were lawyers.

Utilizing the father's occupation as a crude index of class position, there is evidence suggesting that type of practice varies with a lawyer's class origin. While almost half (47 per cent) of the informants whose fathers were skilled or unskilled laborers were in general practice, over two-thirds (69 per cent) of the rest, whose fathers held middle-class occupations, were in concentrated or specialized practices.

A similar pattern emerges from a comparison of law schools attended by these attorneys. As we pointed out before, law schools usually recruit students from different social strata. Given their higher tuition costs and full-time, day-session programs, most university schools draw a greater proportion of students from upper socioeconomic groups than do Catholic and independent schools. Accordingly, 50 per cent of the informants whose fathers were professionals or business executives had attended a university-affiliated law school, and 73 per cent of those whose fathers were small businessmen, white collar workers, or laborers had attended independent or Catholic law schools.

There is also some indication, as others have found, that law school background is related to type of practice.[34] Among lawyers in our sample, one out of four university graduates, as opposed to only one out of ten Catholic and independent School graduates, was engaged in completely specialized practices. In addition, the reported relationship between type of practice and length of time in practice is qualified in one important respect by law school background. The qualification pertains to the probability of a lawyer remaining in general practice. Among university school graduates who were in general practice, the median number of years in practice was 8 years; among the Catholic school graduates it was 19 years; and among graduates of independent schools it was 23 years. With this one exception, there was no significant difference in the length of time in practice among graduates of different law schools. This suggests that while most attorneys may begin their careers as general practitioners, university graduates are not only more likely to specialize but to specialize sooner than graduates of other kinds of schools.

How quickly a lawyer specializes is not, as we have seen, a matter of individual planning, nor is it determined by his law school experience. The processes that differentiate legal practices, though influenced by law schools, do not originate there. Although intelligence, motivation, hard work, "personality," and the demand for legal services all play a part, an attorney's practice, like the type of law school he attended, tends to reflect his class origin. Furthermore, since law practices are established and maintained on the basis of a personal referral system, a lawyer's class background also determines, more often than not, the kinds of clients and cases available to him.

Clients' Class Background

The class backgrounds of clients provide another criterion for distinguishing law practices. Our informants were asked to describe the kinds of people they *normally* represented. An analysis of these descriptions revealed three types of clientele: working class, middle class, and upper class. A working-class clientele refers to one in which most clients are employed in occupations with relatively modest prestige and income. A clientele was coded as working class if an informant, in describing his usual clients, mentioned skilled and unskilled laborers and excluded wealthy individuals. In contrast, an upper-class clientele refers to one in which most clients hold occupational statuses associated with high income and prestige. Clienteles were so classified if an attorney mentioned such individuals, usually corporation executives and their relatives, and excluded manual workers. Finally, clienteles which included neither skilled and un-

Table 1: Clients' Class Background by Attributes of Law Practice, in Per Cent [a]

ATTRIBUTES OF LAW PRACTICE	CLIENTS' CLASS BACKGROUND			
	Upper	Middle	Working	Number of Lawyers
Type of practice				
General	—	10	90	(29)
Concentrated	27	44	29	(41)
Specialized	58	25	17	(12)
Organization of practice [b]				
Solo	19	23	58	(48)
Partnership	26	42	32	(31)
Time in practice				
22 years and less	17	20	63	(41)
23 years and more	27	39	34	(41)
Type of law school attended				
University	41	19	40	(27)
Catholic	15	30	55	(20)
Independent	11	37	52	(35)
Lawyers' fathers' occupations				
Professional and business executive	30	30	40	(20)
Small business and "white collar"	16	35	49	(43)
Skilled and unskilled labor	26	16	58	(19)

[a] Per cents are added horizontally.
[b] Excludes three salaried associates.

skilled workers nor upper-class individuals, but which were composed chiefly of professionals, salesmen, salaried managers, and owners of small or medium-sized business concerns, were designated as middle class.

The relationship between characteristics of law practice and clients' class background is illustrated by the data presented in Table 1. There we see, among other things, that each type of practice tends to serve clients of a particular social stratum. General practitioners show an almost complete reliance on working-class clienteles; those with concentrated practices draw mostly from the middle class, and specialists largely serve the upper class.

As might be anticipated, a clientele's class background relates to other attributes of practice. There is, for example, a general association between a lawyer's class origin and his clients' class position: lawyers whose fathers were professionals or business executives were more apt to have upper-class clients and less likely to have clients from the working class than other attorneys. Similarly, the clients of attorneys who graduated from university law schools were more apt to come from higher social strata than did those of Catholic and independent school graduates. Moreover, the type of clientele varies with length of time in practice and organization of practice. Most informants who had been in practice for 23 years or more, or who were partners, had middle- or upper-class clienteles; most of those with less professional experience, or who were in solo practice, had working-class clients.

The class background of clients affects the practice of law because it is linked to the willingness of individuals to seek legal counsel, their attitudes toward lawyers, their ability to pay for professional help, and the content of their legal problems. In the first place, people do not seek professional aid whenever and simply because they need it. The complex process of defining and handling personal problems is influenced by a variety of cultural and structural variables, among which class position holds a strategic place.[35] This is exemplified by evidence attesting to the fact that many middle- and lower-class individuals have legal problems which they do not take to lawyers.[36] Moreover, to the extent that attorneys draw their clients from these two strata, they are dealing frequently with people who tend to exaggerate and fear the size of legal fees, who would prefer not to share their problems with "outsiders," and who commonly view the lawyer as one who defends those "presumed to have violated the law." [37] In addition, such sentiments probably lessen the significance of whatever referrals members of these classes might make. In a sense the stratification system operates to reduce the number of clients available to attorneys with working- and middle-class clienteles.

Beyond controlling the use of professional services, the class system generates typically different attitudes toward professionals.[38] To be sure, most laymen are somewhat ambivalent toward all professionals. Indeed, it is hard to see how it could be otherwise. On the one hand, with their trained ability to cope with difficult and persistent human problems, professionals are admired and respected; on the other, their monopoly of vitally important knowledge, combined with laymen's inability to evaluate the application of such knowledge, makes professionals vulnerable to public suspicion. This general ambivalence is tempered, however, by class attributes such as educational achievement and financial position.

The lack of much formal education may make it more difficult for a client to comprehend the meaning of legal services. "Education makes it easy," commented one attorney, "easier to explain. Otherwise, we have to go through a rigamarole: explain this, re-explain it and so forth." A poorly educated client may also mistrust what he does not understand, an attitude ascribed by another informant to many of his working-class clients:

> Most of the people I see, lower class people—ignorant, with little education—well, they're real suspicious. They don't trust the opposing lawyer, and they have doubts about their own lawyer.

But ignorance can also breed dependency. Ill-educated clients are less able to judge, let alone challenge, professional legal opinion than those who are better educated. In fact, the latter, as several informants noted, often exercise considerable independence in dealing with attorneys. One lawyer assessed the effect of education on clients' behavior with the following comment:

> The less-educated person is the easiest client. He listens to you, he follows your advice, he looks up to a lawyer. The educated feel that they are just as smart as the lawyer. They listen, but then they figure they can accept or reject your advice.

A client's economic status can have a similar effect on his attitude toward counsel. The rich are less likely to adopt a deferential attitude than are those in less affluent circumstances; in fact, the possession of substantial wealth can lead a client to feel relatively autonomous of law and lawyers. For this reason, attorneys sometimes find it easier to represent clients with average or low incomes. As an informant explained:

> If a man is just an ordinary guy and he consults you, you tell him the law and what can be done, and that's the end of it. If the client has a lot of money, it's more difficult.

You tell him the law, and he doesn't care what the law is. He wants you to do something. That's why he's paying you, and he tells you as much.

Of course a client's financial position does much more than affect his attitude toward lawyers. More significantly, it determines his ability to pay for legal services. This obvious fact means that millions of Americans are unable to hire a lawyer, and that millions more can afford to pay only small fees. To say that social problems and legal inequities flourish under such conditions is no longer novel; but, considering the tragic implications, the assertion is no less relevant today than it was when Reginald Heber Smith publicized it over forty years ago.[39] The organized bar's attempt to remedy the situation, motivated by its fear of "socialism" as by a collective sense of injustice, has left a large segment of the population without access to adequate legal representation. However, our concern here is with the consequences of clients' economic resources on the practice of law. Clearly, legal fees are affected. Lawyers with rich or well-to-do clients can demand relatively high minimum fees and reject clients who cannot meet their demands. As an attorney with an upper-class clientele said: "You tell them what your fee is and that's that. They take it or they don't." Lawyers without wealthy clients have a more flexible policy, and their fees usually are tailored to meet a client's ability to pay. An informant with a working-class clientele commented:

When the clients are working people, you have to get what you can. . . . You charge some more than others, if they have it. You charge generally what the traffic will bear. Some you're overpaid; others, you don't get near enough.

Whatever the fee may be, professionals are expected to render the same quality of service. Nevertheless, it is probably true that, to some unknown degree, the size of legal fees influences the amount of time and effort devoted by lawyers to their cases. In particular, the amount of time spent on legal research may be conditioned by the anticipated compensation. An informant put the issue this way:

To some extent, the fee determines the depth and scope of your research. I don't mean that you neglect a client; not at all. But if you are paid a large fee . . . you really do a bang-up job.

To illustrate his point, this same informant drew our attention to a recently completed brief on his desk:

See that brief in front of you. That's over fifty pages, really exhaustive. . . . My fee here is excellent, so I knocked myself out. Now in the same matter for a more normal fee, I might have done a brief of about twelve pages. The essential points would have been covered, but I wouldn't have done such a thorough job. You have to match your time and hours with the return.

The quality of professional service is not easily judged, even by practitioners. Theoretically, the services offered by each lawyer are unique; in fact, the handling of particular cases varies with an attorney's general intellectual ability, his trained skill, his professional experience, and with the specific problems raised by his client's case. Yet, the size of a fee remains an important, if not always decisive, factor; and a lawyer's use of available legal knowledge pertinent to his client's problem may depend, as the next excerpt states, on his fee.

You know so many of these matters are so small they don't justify much time in research, and even when I know there's a lot to look up. But I've got to eat, and if the matter is small, it doesn't pay you to do much research.

Fees affect an attorney's professional work in still another respect: frequently, they dictate the strategy and tactics employed in legal representation. In giving advice about types of actions, places of jurisdiction, gathering of evidence, negotiation, and litigation, a lawyer must consider carefully his client's finances. Sound professional guidance is useless if a client cannot pay the costs involved. For example, a party's economic status is often a controlling factor in determining the outcome of personal injury suits. Contingent fees aside, many injured plaintiffs cannot afford to wait several years to press their claims in court, and their financial plight plays no small part in the settlement of such cases. In like fashion, the selection of a local or foreign jurisdiction in matrimonial actions depends partly, as we have seen, on clients' economic resources.

Types of Cases

Legal practices can be differentiated further by the types of cases usually handled by practitioners. Consequently, although general practice is marked by a comparative diversity of legal problems, the diversity is limited. In fact, among general practitioners in our sample, the diversity was confined mainly to five kinds of cases: matrimonial, commercial, real estate, negligence, and criminal. Every general practitioner reported at least three of these five as characteristic of his work; eighteen reported four; and nine all five.

The types of cases dealt with by those in concentrated practices take a different form. Sixteen of these attorneys had essentially business practices in which their work was focused on corporate, commercial, or real estate problems. Thirteen others had personal service practices in which they concentrated mostly on criminal, matrimonial, or negligence cases, and a dozen had mixed practices combining some degree of specialization in both business and personal service problems.

There were twelve specialists in our sample. Eight of these devoted themselves exclusively to matrimonial cases. The remaining four specialized in various aspects of business law: two were specialists in corporation law; the third handled only minority stockholder suits, and the fourth confined his practice to the collection of debts for large department stores.

The significance of types of cases for the practice of law becomes apparent if we introduce a distinction which, though not noted explicitly by our informants, has consequences of which they were well aware. In some cases, an attorney is serving a client who requires fairly constant legal advice; in others, a client needs only temporary help. The difference, therefore, between negotiating a commercial contract and a plaintiff's suit in a personal injury case is not just a difference in substantive legal problems. By definition, the commercial client is in some form of business enterprise for which future legal guidance will be needed; he is potentially a permanent client. In contrast, the plaintiff in a tort action is usually a transitory client; his tort problems are not likely to recur with sufficient frequency for him to be viewed by counsel as a permanent client.

Depending on the types of cases handled, a legal clientele can be described as predominantly permanent or transient. The presence of a high proportion of transitory clients would seem to intrude a dimension of uncertainty into practice, for it often is accompanied by irregular income. An informant with a highly diversified personal service practice felt that this was the most onerous feature of his work:

One week you're as busy as you can be, and then you sit around for weeks or months until another busy spell sets in. . . . That's the hardest part of it: your income isn't steady.

In the absence of the security provided by permanent clients, lawyers may be required to look for more regular sources of income outside of law practice. Here are the relevant remarks of an attorney whose practice was confined chiefly to matrimonial and negligence cases:

You may make $5,000 in one month and nothing for the next two months. Meanwhile your expenses continue. It puts the lawyer under a great deal of tension so that you will find many lawyers develop side incomes to take off the pressure. They may get into real estate or insurance, something that will lessen the financial pressure. I'm trying now to sell a TV program.

The distinction between permanent and transitory clients suggests that law practice may be thought of as a community inhabited by clients. In the same way that communities can be classified by their degree of stability, legal practices can be located along a continuum of work stability. And, as a large proportion of permanent residents is required for substantial community cohesion, so a large number of permanent clients would seem to afford the most stable foundation for the practice of law. Aside from regular clients, stability in professional work may be increased through specialization. Insofar as they achieve some reputation in their fields and can count on referrals from other lawyers, specialists have less fluctuating incomes than general practitioners. Thus, even specialization in negligence, matrimonial, and criminal cases may yield sufficient volume to offset the effects of dealing with a nonrepetitive clientele. In any event, general practice, with its heavy reliance on a variety of personal-service legal problems, appears to be the most unstable type of practice, the one least likely to exhibit a steady pattern of cases and fees.

The relationship between stability of work and type of practice may be correlated with that between degree of specialization and freedom to select cases. This may be illustrated by the distribution of lawyers who reported accepting cases that they preferred to reject. Usually, these were cases disliked for personal reasons. The assumption here is that, within limits, the more stable an attorney's practice, the greater his freedom to accept or decline new cases. While half of the informants in general practice said that they took cases they disliked, this was reported by only one-third of those with concentrated practices, and by only one specialist. The reasons given for this behavior are equally instructive. The general practitioners accepted such cases because they could not afford to turn them away. One explained bluntly: "To tell you the truth, I'm in no position to refuse any kind of client." The explanation offered by the specialist and those with concentrated practices was quite different: they dealt with disliked cases as a personal favor to relatives, friends, and past or present clients. Said one of them: "I still have to do things that I would prefer to avoid, an occasional collection matter. But I do it only as a service for a regular client and not because I have to."

The cases lawyers are apt to receive as well as the pressures to accept or reject these cases depend on the structure of their legal practices. Thus, the typology of practice by degree of specialization provides some clue to the kinds of matrimonial practice, and it gives us some intimation of the probable impact of matrimonial cases on each type.

TYPES OF MATRIMONIAL PRACTICE

CHAPTER 4

Every attorney in our sample had at least one matrimonial case during the six-month period preceding our interview with him. That one case, however, was part of a larger configuration of similar cases. An analysis of these configurations revealed three types of practice,[1] each distinguishable from the others by four attributes: (1) the relative frequency with which lawyers were involved in such cases; (2) the degree to which the cases were perceived as a normal part of practice; (3) the major source of referral; and (4) the reasons for accepting the cases. In the following discussion we shall describe each type, relate each to the broader typology of law practice, note the functions served by these cases, and then examine the differential impact of the cultural context on matrimonial practice.

Peripheral Practice

For eighteen informants, cases pertaining to marital dissolutions constituted a negligible part of their professional work. All of these lawyers indicated that the cases were incidental or peripheral to their legal practices. For example, when we inquired how often they participated in matrimonial actions, the answers ranged from one every five years to eighteen a year. However, the majority (ten of the eighteen) estimated that they generally handled less than four such cases each year. More important than these estimates, which are of limited value,[2] was the companion judgment, expressed by every informant, that the cases were comparatively rare. As the next series of comments implies, these lawyers tend to see themselves as practitioners who do not deal with matrimonial problems:

We get about six to ten matrimonial clients a year. . . . We don't do much of it.

We get very few such cases. Maybe one or two a year.

The case I handled recently, you know the one that gave you my name, that was the first in about five years.

I have had about six matrimonial clients in thirty-three years of practice.

As we might expect, the frequency with which an attorney experiences certain types of legal problems affects his perception of his work. Thus, in describing their law practices, thirteen of these lawyers excluded matrimonial cases; and the five who did include them made it clear, through the use of such phrases as "extremely small" and "very little," that the cases were considered to be a fairly insignificant part of practice.

The relatively few cases that appear in peripheral practices are primarily the result of recommendations made by regular business clients. Although one-third of these informants said that they generally received matrimonial cases from their friends and relatives, two-thirds cited their regular clientele as the major source of referral. None reported receiving cases from other lawyers. This pattern of referral has two important consequences that emphasize the marginal position of these cases in peripheral practices. First, the matrimonial cases are chiefly by-products of counsel's nonmatrimonial practice and, to a lesser extent, his nonprofessional relationships. Second, matrimonial clients often are known, sometimes well known, to an attorney beforehand. Therefore, his interests in their problems may be more personal than professional. Said one attorney:

> Most of my marital clients are the children of my regular clients. . . . Their problems become my problems. I'm interested because I've known them from their earliest childhood in many cases. I'm often very friendly with their parents.

If lawyers with peripheral practices participate in comparatively few matrimonial actions, the few are apt to be considered a few too many. Three-fourths of these lawyers expressed a desire to shun even this borderline kind of practice. The comment of one informant, "I'd rather avoid them if I can," aptly characterizes their general sentiment. Why, then, are the cases accepted?

The reason given by these informants for accepting matrimonial cases reveals another distinguishing feature of peripheral practice. Each informant explained his acceptance as a personal service performed for regular clients, or for his own relatives and friends. As the following excerpts indicate, this service is motivated by a sense of obligation to significant role partners, an obligation that takes priority over lawyers' attitudes toward the cases:

We do it for one of our regular clients or for a person recommended by one of the clients. It's really a service we maintain for our clients. But I wish there were a way of not handling them at all.

I don't like them. . . . In all my practice I have had only about four matrimonial cases. . . . In each case, it was a very close friend of the family, and that was the only reason I bothered.

I don't care for them . . . but it's difficult to turn down someone recommended by a friend of mine.

In handling a matrimonial case a lawyer is providing professional service. Why do these attorneys emphasize the personal rather than the professional dimension of their services? The distinction depends on an attorney's relationship to the recommending party. A lawyer's willingness to accept the kind of case that he does not usually handle, and which he would prefer to avoid, is ample testimony that he acknowledges and values his relationship to the referring individual.

The significance of this relationship, in many instances, affects the arrangement of fees. Half of these informants reported that they either undercharged marital clients or handled their cases for no fee. "I don't charge anything," said one, "I do it as a favor to my clients." And another lawyer noted: "Our fees in these matters run between one-half and three-fourths of what it cost us to handle. It's a favor we do for our clients." It should be kept in mind that the recipients of these "favors" are regular clients and not those directly involved in the matrimonial cases.

Minor Practice

For most lawyers in our sample, matrimonial cases were neither marginal nor central to the practice of law. Forty-six informants were engaged in what can be best described as minor matrimonial practices. As a group, these lawyers reported dealing with more matrimonial cases than those with peripheral practices. Again, the numerical estimates are less significant than the general assessment that the cases play a small but important part in practice. Thus, while all of these informants said that they could count on at least one such case a year, twenty-five estimated two to eleven cases, and twenty-one estimated twelve to twenty-five cases a year.

Although these lawyers generally reported greater participation in matrimonial actions than peripheral practitioners, none of them considers himself even partly specialized in this kind of legal problem. However, most of them did recognize that matrimonial cases constituted a definite if minor part of their work; three-fourths of them included the cases in describing their law practices.

A minor practice can be characterized further by its main source of referral. While one-fourth of these informants cited regular clients, and one-fourth mentioned friends and relatives, half of them pointed to their past matrimonial clients as the major source of new cases. One lawyer also said that he occasionally received cases from other members of the bar. The reliance of minor practitioners on the recommendations of previous marital clients does not mean, of course, that the same past clients are involved. As one attorney explained:

Most of my marital cases come from recommendations of other matrimonial clients. . . . I remember one case about six years ago. I'll bet you that I have had about one hundred referrals from that one case. I don't mean that one client sent them all. But each one, in turn, recommends one or two.

In discussing the acceptance of these cases, lawyers with minor practices never referred to the rendering of personal services or "favors." Instead, all of them defined the cases as an opportunity to provide a professional service for a fee. Such cases are, as one informant expressed it, "part of the business, part of my work. And I get paid for it, so I take it." And another lawyer made essentially the same point when he said:

Clients are clients. Matrimonials are bread and butter. It's a question of economics. If I can get a fee and do something for my client, that's it.

Furthermore, none of these attorneys expressed a wish to avoid this type of case. This is not to suggest that they liked the cases; rather, it reflects the "bread-and-butter" view that "clients are clients," a view that attaches more importance to income than to the content of a legal problem. The sentiments of these practitioners was best summed up by the lawyer who stated his feelings about matrimonial cases in these words: "I feel anxious to take them. Take the case and earn the fee is my attitude."

Major Practice

For eighteen of our informants, the legal problems attending separation, annulment, and divorce constituted a major part of their practices. Eight of them were engaged almost exclusively in handling matrimonial cases, while the other ten indicated that their practices were dependent largely, though not exclusively, on these cases. This group reported dealing with more matrimonial actions than other lawyers. Specifically, four of them said that they could count on receiving twenty-five to twenty-nine such cases each year, ten estimated thirty to fifty annual cases, and four indicated fifty or more cases every year. The highest estimate was given by one lawyer who said that he usually handled about one hundred of these actions each year.

This considerable concentration in one field of law was revealed also in the depictions of practice. Each of these lawyers included matrimonial cases in describing his practice, and all but three identified themselves as matrimonial specialists.

Lawyers with major matrimonial practices tend to receive their cases primarily from other attorneys and, secondarily, through the recommendations of past clients. Fourteen gave the former as their major source of referral, while eleven cited the latter. None mentioned their own friends and relatives; only two reported regular clients as a source.[3]

In explaining why such cases were accepted, these informants confirmed the fact that their practices were focused, partly or completely, on this one type of legal problem. For most of them, matrimonial practice was almost synonymous with law practice. "As you can see," said one, "I haven't much choice." But if this specialization implies, by definition, a willingness to accept matrimonial cases, it is by no means the unwilling acceptance of those with peripheral practices, nor is it the "bread-and-butter" acceptance of those with minor practices. On the contrary, all but one of these attorneys expressed a marked preference for such cases. Without exploring now the reasons for this preference,* it is important to note that these cases have a particular meaning for major practitioners, a meaning that affects their preference for legal problems. We refer to the tendency of major practitioners to equate their professional reputations as lawyers with success in matrimonial practice. For example, one attorney commented: "People have heard of me because I've managed to be fairly successful in most of the matrimonial cases I've handled." Furthermore, the reliance of most of these informants on the referrals of other lawyers would seem to substantiate their self-appraisals as successful matrimonial practitioners.

Law Practice and Matrimonial Practice

We suggested before that the larger context of law practice would exercise a strong control over the type of matrimonial practice engaged in by lawyers, that different kinds of legal practice would be accompanied by specific patterns of matrimonial practice. The data in hand clearly illustrate this broad relationship. Among our twenty-nine informants in general practice, twenty-seven had minor matrimonial practices. Among the non-general practitioners, the type of matrimonial practice varied with the type of specialization. Of the twenty-five attorneys who concentrated or specialized in business cases, fifteen had peripheral and ten had minor matrimonial practices; of the nineteen lawyers whose work was focused on personal service cases, twelve had major and seven had minor matrimonial practices. In brief,

* Lawyers' preference for designated types of cases is related to their over-all conceptions of the professional role. These conceptions are examined at length in Chapter 6.

peripheral matrimonial practices are associated with business practices, minor matrimonial practices with general practice, and major matrimonial practices with personal service practices.

In discussing the relationship between law practice and matrimonial actions, we need to comment further on major matrimonial practices. To point out that lawyers who concentrate on personal service cases often have major matrimonial practices comes close to asserting a tautology. We can look, however, at this kind of practice from a different perspective by raising the query: How do lawyers become specialists in matrimonial cases?

Characteristically, informants with major matrimonial practices never intended to specialize in these cases. Instead, the process of specialization occurred mainly through unforeseen developments in which they found themselves dealing with an increasing number of marital actions. A few examples ilustrate this pattern. Here is one lawyer's description of how his practice emerged:

> I like matrimonial cases, but I didn't have this as my goal. About seven or eight years ago my partner and I discussed the problem of practice and found that we had been doing a great deal of matrimonial work. So we thought we'd try and specialize in it. We passed along the word to our friends in the profession and elsewhere that we were eager to do this kind of work. So now that's our specialty.

Another informant gave us this brief history of his practice:

> Before World War II, I was starving like many lawyers. Then, during the war, I did a lot of work on a legal committee to help servicemen at a nominal or no fee. In that capacity I handled thousands of matrimonial matters of one kind or another. As a result I got a lot of referrals after the war and stayed in it.

Still another lawyer told us that during his fifth year of practice he had quite a few matrimonial cases. He gathered the legal notes he had collected for those cases and published several articles and a book. These publications brought him more matrimonial cases, and he decided to make the field his specialty. Finally, here is an account of the effect of a "big case":

I never planned to specialize in these matters, but back in 1952 I was called into a case in Nassau County by a lawyer who felt it was hopeless. It was a matrimonial involving people who had a good deal of wealth. The odds were against us but we finally won. The case received a great deal of publicity in the papers, and, as a result, I got a lot of them, and have been in it ever since.

Four themes are discernible in similar descriptions of matrimonial specialization: (a) as we have indicated, the specialization was unplanned; (b) a sequence of matrimonial cases emerged in the course of practice; (c) the cases were perceived as a potential specialty; (d) active efforts were made to encourage the referral of other similar cases. In rough outline, this process probably is approximated in the development of most specialized legal practices. But this process is affected by at least two other important considerations. First, the kinds of cases a lawyer receives, particularly during the early part of his career, is governed partly by his nonprofessional characteristics. Thus, although attorneys are prone to view specialization as a product of fortuitous events in practice, the *types* of events that they are likely to experience are influenced by their social background. For example, it is unlikely that lawyers of high socioeconomic origin will encounter many criminal, matrimonial, or negligence cases. Since they are more apt to be employed by large law firms than those from lower social strata, and since these firms are concerned primarily with business problems, the kind of cases and the types of specialties accordingly are restricted. Correlatively, it is unlikely that attorneys with a working-class background, usually graduates of evening law schools starting out as independent practitioners, will handle, let alone specialize in, problems of corporate reorganization. The process of specialization may be similar for most lawyers, but the fields of specialization are not equally available to all.

The process of legal specialization is affected by a second factor: lawyers personal preferences for certain kinds of cases. We noted before that legal practices often undergo specialization in specific problems. The decision to encourage further specialization is contingent, to some degree, on a personal preference. An attorney is not apt to specialize continuously in a field of law that he dislikes; not, at least, if he can help it. On the other hand, a lawyer who persists in restricting his practice to a particular field, who comes to think of himself as a specialist in that field, and who is so identified by others, is apt to prefer some aspect of his specialty.

Functions of Matrimonial Cases

These findings about matrimonial practice are important because they provide a strategic insight into the practice of law: the same type of legal problem has different consequences for different types of practitioners. The significance of matrimonial cases for lawyers varies, therefore, from one kind of legal practice to another. More specifically, the cases serve diverse functions in different types of law practice.

The primary function of a matrimonial case in general practice is to furnish counsel with a supplementary source of income. Because he depends on no one type of legal problem, a general practitioner is dependent on all types, or at least all that he can obtain. As a result of the diverse nature of his work, he is likely to receive a limited number of several types of cases, none of which he can afford to refuse. In this situation, a matrimonial case is neither indispensable nor irrelevant; rather, it plays a small but important part in supporting an attorney's practice. Essentially the same function is served by other kinds of cases. Thus, it is the cumulative impact of various legal problems—matrimonial plus criminal plus collections, and so forth—that produces some semblance of security in general practice.

In legal practices that are concentrated or specialized in business problems, matrimonial cases serve a different function: they tend to sustain the relationship between an attorney and his regular clientele. Obviously, this relationship is necessary in order to maintain a business practice. Under these conditions the fee in a matrimonial case is of secondary concern to lawyers. What is important, however, is the opportunity to serve clients in a personal capacity and thereby strengthen the bond between attorneys and clients. As was pointed out, the relationship at stake here is not that of lawyer and matrimonial client, but of a lawyer to the referring party, his regular client. Attorneys may be motivated in accepting matrimonial cases recommended by business clients for various reasons: they may feel grateful for past legal work, anxious about receiving future cases, or they may act out of feelings of friendship. At any rate, whatever their motives, the effect of taking a case is the same: it tends to maintain positive sentiments between lawyers and their actual or potential clients whose legal problems constitute the core of business practice. If the function of a matrimonial case in general practice is primarily economic, in business practice its function its mainly integrative.

For lawyers who spend a substantial amount of their professional time handling matrimonial actions, these cases serve three related functions, none of which is found in other types of practice. First, such cases supply most of these attorneys with a principal, and in some instances sole, source of legal income. Second, the cases influence their professional self-image; they tend to think of themselves as matrimonial practitioners. Third, the cases provide other members of the bar with an image that identifies these attorneys as specialists. When this perception by others actually leads to referrals, it reinforces a specialist's self-image and, of course, contributes to his income.

The Impact of the Cultural Context

In Chapter 2 we described the cultural context of matrimonial practice in New York. The context, it will be remembered, involves a discrepancy between public sentiments about the termination of marriage and legal norms regulating such dissolutions. The combination of these conflicting cultural items poses a problem for lawyers: they must serve their clients without evading their professional responsibility to support the law. But this problem does not confront all lawyers; the cultural context does not have the same impact on all members of the bar. Although this observation may be self-evident, it implies a less obvious and more significant generalization: the effect of the cultural context on professional behavior is mediated by the structure of law practice. Because they engage in different types of legal practice, attorneys have different kinds of matrimonial practices; and as these latter practices vary, so does exposure to the cultural context.

The differential impact of the cultural context can be illustrated by examining the choice of jurisdiction in divorce cases. Confronted with clients who wish to obtain a divorce, attorneys usually have two alternatives: they can advise that residency be established and an action initiated in a jurisdiction outside of New York; or they can advise that the proceedings take place locally. If the foreign jurisdiction is chosen, the problems created by the cultural conflict are circumvented. If the action is local, then both lawyer and client must accommodate to the New York context. To be sure, this decision will rest, in part, on the evidence in each case. But, for our purposes, this factor can be ignored. We are more interested in any characteristic of law practice that might predispose an attorney, whatever the evidence may be, to advise consistently one jurisdiction rather than another.

The socioeconomic background of a legal clientele is precisely this kind of characteristic. Since the costs of travel to, and residence in, a foreign jurisdiction are greater than the costs of securing a local divorce, a client's financial resources probably determine, in most cases, where the divorce will be secured. Consequently, we would expect that the frequency with which a lawyer is involved in New York matrimonial actions is largely determined by his clients' class position.

We asked our informants where most of their matrimonial clients obtained their divorces. Many lawyers had difficulty in answering this question. Some claimed that it was impossible to classify their practices by jurisdiction.[4] Others, curiously enough, took the position that since it was a violation of legal ethics to suggest a foreign divorce, the query was unfair.[5] Among the forty-five informants who did describe their divorce cases by place of jurisdiction, we find the following patterns: only one out of fourteen peripheral practitioners, and only two out of nine major practitioners reported that their clients' divorce actions usually took place in New York; in contrast, fifteen out of twenty-two minor practitioners said that they handled most of their divorce cases in local courts. It would appear, then, that attorneys with minor matrimonial practices are more likely than other lawyers to be exposed directly to the New York cultural context. But who are these minor practitioners? As we indicated above, they are mostly general practitioners who, it will be recalled, usually have working-class clienteles.

Further evidence bearing on the association between a minor practice and clients with relatively low socio-economic status appears in a comparison of types of matrimonial practice with clients' class background. Almost three-fourths (74 per cent) of lawyers with minor matrimonial practices had working-class clienteles. In contrast, 22 per cent of those with major practices and only 11 per cent of those with peripheral practices normally had clients from the working class.

The tendency for minor practitioners to use local rather than foreign jurisdictions seems clearly to be related to a specific attribute of law practice: the working-class background of their clients. As one lawyer remarked about his matrimonial clients: "They all go through the local courts. They can't afford to travel." This selection of jurisdiction is supported by the economic function served by matrimonial cases in this type of practice. Several minor practitioners stated their preference for local actions on the grounds that their fees would be larger than in a foreign proceeding, where another lawyer would have to be retained. "I prefer that they go in New York," explained one attorney, "because I don't have to split the fee."

In a similar fashion, the jurisdiction chosen by lawyers with peripheral and major matrimonial practices is influenced by their clientele's class attributes. Since their clients come from comparatively high socioeconomic strata, there are normally fewer financial obstacles to obtaining divorces outside of New York. Nor, given the clients' relative affluence, are these lawyers apt to be motivated to pursue local actions in order to receive higher fees. Furthermore, the occupational statuses of these clients may raise a problem of notoriety, an issue not likely to be as relevant for members of the working class. A foreign divorce may be desirable, as the next excerpt indicates, as an expedient way of protecting clients against adverse publicity:

> Well, it's more expensive to go out of state, but . . . it's a matter of reputation. If it's local, the newspapers can get hold of the story and report it first hand. . . . A client may be a well-known businessman, and he doesn't want that kind of publicity.

This short discussion of jurisdiction in divorce cases exemplifies an important generalization: the degree to which social behavior is affected by a surrounding cultural milieu is controlled by intervening structural variables. As we have just seen, whether or not lawyers are consistently exposed to the cultural conflict between New York matrimonial laws and public opinion depends on a structural attribute of their legal practices, in this instance, their clients' class background.

PROFESSIONAL IMAGES OF MATRIMONIAL CASES

CHAPTER 5

We have examined different types of legal practices and have learned something of the ways in which they are related to different kinds of matrimonial practice. We noted, in particular, that the significance of marital cases for a lawyer varies with the context of his practice. We now need to look at these cases as they are perceived and evaluated by lawyers. This should enable us to understand how attorneys are affected by the distinctive—though as we shall see, far from exclusive—characteristics of matrimonial cases. Some insight into these characteristics is provided by the various attributes reported by the lawyers we interviewed. They talked freely about their past and present marital cases and often drew comparisons with other types of legal problems. In brief, they presented their professional imagery of matrimonial cases. Table 2 summarizes the array of images obtaining among the eighty-two informants.

Table 2: Lawyers' Images of Matrimonial Cases, in Per Cent [a]

Emotionally upset clients	74
Clients ignorant of law	37
Strain on lawyer	28
Female clients	27
Personal problems	23
Involvement of lawyer	17
Nonlegal problems	16
Number of lawyers	82

[a] Each lawyer mentioned several images which accounts for the percentages far exceeding one hundred.

The reported professional images fall into three categories: (1) attributes of clients, (2) dimensions of matrimonial problems, and (3) effects of the cases on lawyers. Furthermore, the frequency with which the different images was reported varied by types of matrimonial practice.

In the discussion that follows we shall describe each image, examine its component parts, locate its source, note its effects on the professional-client relationship, compare it with attributes of other kinds of cases, and look at its variation among different types of practitioners. We shall then report our informants' attitudes toward matrimonial cases.

The Matrimonial Client

1. Client-Emotionalism Foremost among the qualities attributed to matrimonial cases by lawyers—irre-

spective of their types of marital practice—is the emotionalism of the client.[1] The 74 per cent of our informants who referred to this characteristic did so at length and with considerable affect. The image of emotionalism is an amalgam of sentiments and behavior which our informants associate with matrimonial clients. The references to client-feelings varied in detail, but the general picture emerging from an analysis of the interview material uniformly portrays individuals responding to stressful situations. Here are a few representative excerpts:

> Matrimonial clients are most subjective, tense, excited . . . unobjective, frightened. . . . They lack confidence.
>
> They are emotional and excited. . . . Their emotions, their lives are all involved. . . . They are acrimonious.
>
> They are in a complete turmoil.
>
> They feel that the world has given them a wrong deal. They feel they've been stuck. They are temporarily upset.

Similarly, the reported behavior of these clients reveals reactions to stress. We were informed of clients who "can't make decisions," who "change their minds," who "make outrageous demands." Many informants illustrated their images of emotional behavior with examples from their own experiences. One lawyer recalled a husband who "wanted to support his children on fifty cents a day"; another remembered a wife "who slashed all the tires on her husband's car"; and still another told of a client who held up an attractive legal settlement until her husband returned a cherished postcard. These, and other similar descriptions of the sentiments and actions of marital clients, were offered by attorneys to substantiate their image of client-emotionalism.[2]

The image of the emotional client clearly resembles

clinical discussions of individual reactions to threatening stimuli.[3] And, as students of American family life have observed, it is unlikely that many people can experience the dissolution of their marriages without some sense of personal disorganization.[4] The structure of modern marriage, established and sustained on a voluntary basis of mutual attraction, and entered into with the normative anticipation of a lifelong partnership, is invested with substantial emotional significance by husband and wife. The process of conflict, culminating in the termination of this highly affective relationship, probably subjects most spouses to a substantial degree of frustration, evoking the familiar mechanisms of adjustment. The problem of adjusting to this kind of situation is made more difficult because the conclusion of a marriage seldom eradicates the mutual attachment once felt. Indifference is not apt to be the modal response; on the contrary, husbands and wives are likely to have feelings of ambivalence which may elicit a pattern of compulsive alienation. The former marriage becomes, to some extent, a negative reference group toward which the ex-spouses are dependently hostile.[5]

Many of our informants were aware of the social and psychological sources of their clients' emotionalism. It was taken for granted that dissolving a marriage was a painful process, and that the accompanying emotional distress was a normal reaction to a difficult situation. Here are three excerpts exemplifying this attitude:

Things have gone very badly for matrimonial clients, and *naturally* they are quite upset.

These clients feel and act like the world has come to an end. And, *in a way, it has for them.*

They are very disturbed emotionally and *for good reason.*

Whatever else lawyers had to say about the emotionalism of matrimonial clients, they did not dismiss it as inappropriate.

To describe an individual as emotionally upset is to do more than communicate information about his subjective condition; it also alerts others to the possible social effects of his psychological state. Our informants reported three consequences of emotionalism that affect a lawyer's relationship with matrimonial clients:

1. Their intense emotional state leads many marital clients to exhibit in acute form a typical characteristic: a partisan apperception of their legal problems. "Clients in general have trouble seeing the other side of the case, but it is most pronounced in marital cases." As far as many husbands and wives are concerned, "they are always 100 per cent right and the adversary 100 per cent wrong." This extreme partisanship makes it difficult for lawyers to explain the importance of "give and take" in legal negotiations: "They think that something's wrong with a lawyer who compromises."

2. The threat to self-esteem motivates many clients to seek vengeance. "They don't just want to dissolve the marriage," commented one attorney, "they want revenge, to get even." A vindictive client does not make a lawyer's job any easier; such clients, "in their efforts to ruin the spouse, very often ruin their own cases."

3. Finally, matrimonial clients, acting under stress, convinced that justice is on their side, and hoping for revenge, tend to look to their lawyers for complete support. They want counsel, we were told, to share their sentiments: "to be bitter," "to hate as they hate," "to have the same grievances toward the spouse as they have." And they prefer that these feelings be manifested in action:

The one thing they all want is for the lawyer to shoot the other side. They'd like it if we went after the other side with a knife, a blade. Then they'd be happy.

The demand for extreme partisan representation exceeds the professional obligation requiring a lawyer to represent his client with zeal; it calls, rather, for an *identification* of the lawyer with his client's point of view. Should a lawyer comply, this would deprive the client of valuable advice based on professional detachment. As our informants noted, the demand conflicts with the objective attitude so necessary for professional work. Said one: "In order to do your job you have to be objective, but this matrimonial clients don't want."

Client-emotionalism, whatever burdens it may put on a lawyer, is not unaffected by the lawyer's behavior. Faced with a distraught spouse, an attorney can offer support and reassurance.[6] "When a marital client comes in here," explained an informant, "the first thing that is called for is kindness and sympathy. That's what they want and need. Then you need to be calm and get them calm." To calm a client, that is, to reduce the effects of emotionalism, an attorney's willingness to listen may be especially effective:

You have to let them get it off their chest. Let them talk to you. When they blow off about their troubles long enough, they feel better; and sometimes they are better able to see what can be done. . . . That's where a lawyer can help; by letting them talk.

An attorney needs, of course, to do more than listen if he is to help his client. Among other things, he must obtain the relevant facts. He must inquire about the marriage and discuss with the client the pattern of conflict that precipitated legal action. But this procedure, indispensable though it is, requires the client to catalogue real or fancied grievances. Thus, in his effort to get necessary information, a lawyer runs the risk of increasing the client's emotional distress. This aspect of professional role behavior was summarized by one lawyer:

> I need to know the facts and in digging them up, in going back over their marriage, the facts are refreshed in the client's mind. They begin to remember how bad things were. In other words, going over the facts often makes the situation worse.

There is another aspect of professional behavior that tends to aggravate client-emotionalism. New York legal procedure in matrimonial cases has one requirement which, according to our informants, almost always insures an increase in the mutual hostility of participating parties. The courts insist that when a plaintiff, through an attorney, moves for temporary alimony and counsel fees, evidence of *probable* success in the anticipated action must be offered. This requirement directly affects the manner in which an attorney will present his client's version of the facts:

> You have to show probability of success. So this means that the lawyer must encourage the client to put things in as drastic a light as possible.

What this procedural norm does, in effect, is to force a lawyer to overstate his client's case; and since the grounds for maintaining an action rest on the principle of fault, the resulting motion generally contains affidavits carefully specifying, frequently in vivid detail, the alleged wrongdoing of the defendant. Plainly, these affidavits are not apt to lessen the emotionalism characteristically found in such cases. Detailed charges elicit detailed denials and even more detailed countercharges.

Most of the informants recognized that the net effect of the probability-of-success norm generally heightens the animosity between husband and wife.[7] "That's why you get so much bitterness in these cases," said one. "They are upset to begin with, but these affidavits and counter-affidavits make the matters worse." Yet, to protect his client, a lawyer must comply with the norm:

I know the other lawyer is going to allege certain things, or I may have his papers and am faced with giving answers. How far should I go in answering them? A simple denial may be enough, but it may not be enough. We may get a judge who reads the dirty allegations of the other side. He may not like what he reads but there it is. Then he reads my answers: simple denials. Is that enough? Can I take the chance? Generally, no. So I have to write an answer that will do a thorough job for my client, and it may not be a pleasant answer.

It is probable that the substance of these affidavits, or at least a reasonable approximation, has already been expressed *privately* between the parties before legal proceedings are initiated. However, the *public* nature of a legal action alters the character of any accusation, and in these cases further intensifies the mutual resentment:

A man can call his wife a tramp, and she can talk about his infidelity. But when it becomes *official*—*public*—by swearing out an affidavit where everything is spelled out word by word, then the temperatures start to rise.

So far we have examined the image of emotionalism and some of its effects on the professional-client relationship. We also noted that many lawyers seem to be aware of the determinants of the emotionalism and how it is influenced by their own behavior. It is therefore paradoxical to find that every informant who mentioned the image also indicated that matrimonial clients did not act like ordinary people. Consider, for example, the following representative remarks:

Marital clients are under terrible tension. They lose the ability to be adult and correct in their judgment.

They are so emotional and excited that they can't see things in the right perspective.

The heat is so severe that they don't know what they are doing.

Such observations imply that the pressure of marital conflict produces behavior that is not quite normal. In the explicit words of one attorney: "No man or woman acts normally when they have a domestic problem." Apparently, normal behavior, in the context of the lawyer-client relationship, means behavior that would occur in the absence of tension, behavior that would be amenable to counsel's rational advice. But, as so many of our informants reported, most matrimonial clients are under considerable tension, and their thoughts, words, and deeds are correlatively somewhat less than normal. What is particularly significant, however, is the tendency of lawyers to classify this type of behavior as nonrational:

People in matrimonial cases are not rational. They're hostile to their own interests. They're irrational.

They don't look at it logically or rationally. They demand instead of thinking. They're emotional and so unrealistic.

The characterization of matrimonial clients as individuals who will not, or cannot, act and think rationally suggests that lawyers lack the skill to cope successfully with these clients. Unlike psychiatrists, marriage counselors, and social workers, lawyers are not usually trained to handle emotional problems. Therefore they find, as one informant expressed it, that "it's difficult to deal with a person who is so upset." The difficulty encountered in representing an "upset" client reflects something more than a lack of training; it also indicates the inappropriateness of *legal* skills, skills based on an objective and logical appraisal of problems:

You can't use logic in matrimonial matters.

It's very hard to get marital clients to be objective.

They're too emotional and just plain unable to listen to reason.

In dealing with matrimonial cases, then, lawyers appear to suffer from what has been aptly identified as "trained incapacity": their skills function as inadequacies.[8]

The description of matrimonial clients as mentally ill supports our inference about trained incapacity. Fourteen lawyers in the sample attributed the actions of these clients to basic personality disorders. Here are three expressions of this view:

The matrimonial client is not the usual client. . . . *They're psychotic.* There's something missing in their behavior.

They are *neurotic, ill* people, people with *profound personality problems.*

Matrimonial clients are *mentally ill* people. They've lost perspective and objectivity.

That some proportion of matrimonial clients may be neurotic or psychotic is probably true and irrelevant. Some proportion of maladjusted personalities can be found in any group of individuals. What is relevant, however, is the judgment of some lawyers who, like many laymen, are prone to identify irrational behavior as abnormal. Such judgments derive from an inability to understand "irrational" behavior except by interpreting it as abnormal. Star's observations, based on a recent study of a national sample's attitudes toward mental illness, bear directly on this point. She reports that "the popular conception of the normal person is that he is highly rational, completely able to control himself, and completely responsible for his acts; and that these acts are always reasonable, appropriate to the circumstances, and intelligible to others in light of the circumstances." She goes on to add: "People do not regard behavior as mental illness unless it represents an almost complete loss of cognitive functioning, unless it is so unreasonable and inappropriate that it cannot be explained in any other way." [9] Thus, when some of our informants characterized marital clients as mentally ill, they were indicating the irrelevancy of their training and skills for the task at hand.[10]

Although matrimonial clients were described as emotional, they obviously share the attribute with other types of clients. It would be an exceptional case that did not arouse some degree of feeling among the participants. Nor were our informants claiming that nonmarital cases are devoid of emotionalism. Since to practice law is to be continuously involved with what one attorney called "the aggravations of people," a lawyer is never far removed from emotional disputes.

If all clients are potentially emotional, what distinguishes the potential of the matrimonial client? The answer lies in the *personal* nature of the latter's problem. An informant made the following comparison with other cases:

The claimant in a negligence action may be angry, and the man who is closing a real estate deal may be apprehensive, but these marital ones are usually *deeper emotional problems.*

As the phrase, "deeper emotional problems," implies, conflict attending the dissolution of marriage is more likely to concern the private aspects of a client's personality than other kinds of legal actions. Hence, as another lawyer noted, "a man may be in a negligence suit and it doesn't tell you anything about him as a person, but in matrimonial cases it often means that something is wrong." The "something" that is "wrong" involves controversy among individuals who are related in familial roles:

A commercial client gets emotional too, but it is about his money. But in matrimonial cases, *other people—husbands, children, and in-laws—are involved.*

In a negligence case, the client has a grievance against a stranger and is out to get some money. In a matrimonial, the client is not merely interested in making money; *he has a grievance against a family* member.

It is, then, the highly interpersonal context that distinguishes the marital client's emotionalism from that of other clients, a context in which past attachments can produce and sustain a present animosity unlike that found in most legal cases.[11] In matrimonial actions, the parties do not represent impersonal organizations, nor are they strangers fighting over property; they are individuals terminating a once meaningful relationship. Unlike most opposing clients, they inflame their feelings with the combustible debris of broken intimacy.

2. CLIENT-IGNORANCE Another image of matrimonial cases reported by lawyers refers to the *ignorance* of clients. This attribute, cited by slightly more than one-third of the informants, covers three related types of ig-

norance: (a) inadequate knowledge of law; (b) misconceptions of a lawyer's role; and (c) vacillation regarding anticipated legal action.

The image of a client's ignorance of law is the more striking when we consider the obvious fact that most clients, marital or not, are laymen. Nevertheless, as the following excerpts show, this commonplace is part of the professional imagery of these cases:

> Matrimonial clients don't understand that the quibbles and quarrels of the marriage do not constitute evidence. What they call cruelty is not necessarily the legal definition of cruelty.
>
> They have misconceptions about so many things—the length of time it will take to do something, the laws in different states—just everything.
>
> Why must they do this or that? Why is the law that way? They just don't understand.

For laymen to be ignorant of the law is hardly a novelty for lawyers; and to be informed that marital clients "are not aware of the legal technicalities" comes as no surprise. What makes this ignorance significant is its relation to a client's understanding of counsel's role. To be ignorant of the law is to be ignorant of the norms that control a lawyer's professional behavior.

Whatever else the public image of a lawyer may be, it probably includes a picture of a professional who helps people solve their legal problems. However, an attorney's ability to aid clients is circumscribed by law in two important respects. First, as an individual practitioner, he cannot alter the legal framework within which his client's problem must be solved. The substantive and procedural parts of this framework constitute the conditions under which a lawyer functions; indeed, they provide the major institutionalized mechanisms for the solution of conflict. Second, many aspects of a lawyer's relationship to his client are defined in statutory and common law and subject to further qualifications by a legally binding code of ethics. Irrespective of a given client's problem, an attorney's services are always constrained, in form and content, by law.[12] Individuals who are ignorant of law are likely to be ignorant of these constraints and, as clients, may have expectations concerning a lawyer's role that are incompatible with those held by members of the profession.

That ignorance of the law generates such expectations in matrimonial cases is evident from our interviews. For the most part, these expectations appear to derive from a public image of the lawyer as one who manipulates the law to meet clients' needs. If, for example, spouses are told by counsel that they have no evidence for a divorce, "they expect you to make up evidence for them." Or, if they wish to hide their actual financial status in order to influence alimony negotiations, "they don't understand why a lawyer won't cooperate with them to conceal the true amount of money they may be worth." As these expectations imply, parties to marital actions often view the lawyer as one who can ignore or alter the legal framework, that it is his job to do so:

> They don't understand that it is not enough that they know something happened. They must have proof, be able to prove it in court. They want to know why can't the lawyer do something.

This client-orientation readily adapts itself to the belief that attorneys are responsible for what clients view as deficiencies in the law. This is, reportedly, the inference drawn by many matrimonial clients who, as one informant explained, "tend to blame defects or delays in the law on the lawyer. 'What's holding up the matter?' they ask. I tell them, 'The law.' But they doubt it." Another attorney, after describing a client's marital problem for which there was no legal remedy, went on to say: "The client can't understand it, and her friends ask her, 'What kind of a lawyer have you got?' I can't change the law. I feel sorry for her, but my hands are tied."

As the last excerpt pointed out, and as other informants noted, matrimonial clients not only tend to hold lawyers accountable for "defects" in the law, they also equate legal ability with "doing something" about the law. Because their general legal ignorance makes it difficult for them to assess legal talent by professional standards, they are apt to apply their own yardstick of accomplishment: [13]

They must have this or that, and if you don't get it for them, it's because you're not a good lawyer.

Faced with this kind of lay judgment, lawyers do not find it easy to explain either the law or their own behavior. To proffered legal explanations, these clients respond, not with comprehension or acceptance, but with the unaltered conviction that a lawyer still ought to do something. They want results, not knowledge:

I explain the law, the requirements of the law, the procedures of the courts, but they still don't truly comprehend. . . . They don't understand why we, the lawyers, can't do something about the whole business.

If they have trouble understanding the legal dimensions of their problems, many marital clients find it impossible to recognize the legitimacy of the opposition. And should their lawyers, in an attempt to explain the law, suggest that the opposing side is entitled to certain rights, they may feel betrayed. "If you try and explain to them anything about the rights of the other side," said one attorney, "you're in trouble. They think you're going to settle behind their backs or sell them out in some way." Anticipating just such misunderstanding and misinterpretation, lawyers may be hesitant to discuss the legal rights of the opposing spouse, sometimes even to the point of withholding complete information about the adversary's legal position and being less than candid in explaining its implications.

> If we try and suggest that it can't be all one-sided, that the other side has some rights, they want to know who are we representing. *So you have to be careful. You can't be candid with them.*

In making this kind of adjustment, a lawyer may be choosing the lesser of two evils: an uninformed client is preferable to one who doubts counsel's integrity. Nevertheless, the reluctance to be candid probably reinforces the client's general legal ignorance.

From a professional point of view, all clients are ignorant, although in varying degrees. Laymen whose occupations require frequent legal advice acquire some legal knowledge and appreciation of what a lawyer can and cannot accomplish. For most people, however, a legal action is a novel event; not infrequently, this action is a matrimonial case. As our informants recognized, the lack of legal experience constitutes the major source of a matrimonial client's ignorance: "The average marital client is only in court once, with his marital case. It's the only time he deals with a lawyer."

In addition to their legal inexperience, many matrimonial clients possess false information of their legal rights and obligations and correlatively false conceptions of a lawyer's role. With the help of gossip and rumor, inexperienced clients may augment their ignorance by drawing fallacious conclusions from fallible information concerning other people's cases. Relatives, friends, and acquaintances can be counted on to put at the disposal of a spouse a collective body of pseudolegal knowledge. Our informants were well aware of this process:

> You find that matrimonial clients are out talking and getting advice from everyone they know who has been through a similar experience. Everyone is playing Perry Mason.

> When it comes to matrimonial law, everyone's an expert. So they all give advice to my client.

> Marital clients get coached by people who had a similar problem, or knew someone who did, and they come back in here with the wildest ideas.

The mass media, by providing a daily diet of matrimonial news from which a client may select and digest morsels of legal lore, perform a similar function. "The newspaper readers," said an attorney, "have read all about the divorces of others and are apt to have a distorted notion of what they can get from a spouse."

Of course matrimonial clients are not alone in their lack of legal experience any more than they are unique in their possession of pseudolegal knowledge. In fact, the preceding discussion could apply to any type of client who does not use legal services frequently. There is, however, another aspect to a marital client's ignorance that is not generally found in other types of cases. In matrimonial actions, clients are often ignorant of their own intentions.[14] As one exasperated informant put it: "They don't know what they want, they change their minds, and consequently, you have to be careful with them."

The possibility of a reconciliation is one major reason for clients' uncertainty. Although legal action is contemplated and counsel retained for that purpose, there may be an alternating pattern of reconciliation and separation. Here is one illustration:

Marital clients have such changes of heart. Some months ago a woman called me and said she wanted a separation from her husband. Well, a week later she told me they were back together again. Then, three weeks later, she and he came in to draw up a separation, which I began to do. They called me last week: they're back together again.

This pattern of client-behavior puts lawyers in a particularly ambivalent position. Though most of them believe that a lawyer should make some effort at reconciliation, they rarely expect their efforts to be successful.* In fact, as we shall see later, many of them take the client's appearance in a law office as evidence that the marriage is over. Meanwhile, they must be prepared to adjust their handling of such cases to the latest shift in clients' plans.

Aside from the possibility of reconciliation, the problem of client uncertainty is complicated further by another kind of behavior: some matrimonial clients hide from counsel their actual reasons for seeking legal help. A client, for instance, may hire an attorney ostensibly to contest an action for divorce when he is actually testing his spouse's determination to dissolve their marriage. One informant bitterly recalled the case in which he was asked by a young husband, who was "deeply in love with his wife," to oppose her attempt to divorce him. This was done successfully, and then, in the lawyer's words:

I called the young man and said that I thought his wife's case had fallen apart. So the next day he came into my

* The problem of reconciliation is discussed in the next chapter.

office and told me that he loved his wife so much that if she wanted a divorce he'd let her have it. . . . Now I ask you, what am I suppose to do?

In other instances, we were told, clients ask lawyers to initiate separation or divorce actions with the hope—not communicated to counsel—that a reconciliation will be effected. This paradoxical maneuver was illustrated by another informant:

I had a recent case where I represented the wife and she really wanted me to go after her husband. . . . We pestered the guy continuously. Then I found out that she was sleeping with the guy. What she really wanted was to get her husband back and this was her way of doing it. She had no intention of divorcing the man. She fooled me. This turns up quite a bit in matrimonial cases.

Knowledge of a client's intentions is particularly important to lawyers in matrimonial cases because they have no other compass to guide their professional efforts. In other types of cases clients may be uncertain, but there are usually some rough rules that an attorney can follow. A lawyer, who complained that in many matrimonial cases "you never know what the client wants," went on to make this comparison:

Now in drafting a will you know where you stand; the thing is pretty clear. I don't mean there are no problems. But a man comes in and wants to draw up a will and you know what's to be done.

Legal problems can be thought of, as this last excerpt suggests, as having more or less built-in guide lines for practitioners. In some cases, a lawyer knows "what's to be done"; in others, he does not unless given specific instructions by clients. An attorney's job would seem to be fairly well structured in criminal and tort actions.

In defending clients charged with crime, he seeks acquittal or minimum punishment for his client; in tort suits he usually strives for a financial verdict or settlement most beneficial to his client. In both types of cases extremely difficult decisions may remain, but there are at least broad criteria that a lawyer can take for granted. Equivalent standards are probably present in most commercial and corporate cases. In contrast, matrimonial actions have no inherent signposts for lawyers to follow except those provided by the parties. Matrimonial clients, to be sure, often do make known their intentions. But, and this is the point made by our informants, just as frequently they do not; or if they do, they change their minds. In the presence of this vacillation, lawyers themselves are uncertain of their clients' best interests. Here is a compact statement of the dilemma given by one attorney:

> In most cases you handle for a client, you usually know what the client wants. For example, in commercial transactions your man is out to make money and you usually try and do things in such a way that will profit him. The point is you have a general guide. You may not get what you want, but you know the direction in which things are moving. *Now there are no such guides in matrimonial work.* Your client is often unsure of anything except breaking the marriage bond. Then they change their minds. And then it's difficult to be sure what is best for the client.

The frequency with which informants associated client-ignorance with matrimonial cases varied with their types of matrimonial practice. A relatively small proportion of those engaged in peripheral and major practices—17 and 11 per cent, respectively—referred to it. On the other hand, client-ignorance was mentioned by slightly more than half (54 per cent) of those with minor practices; for these lawyers the attribute was almost as salient as client-emotionalism. The fact that minor practitioners have a greater proportion of working-class clients than other practitioners probably accounts for the differential in perception. With a limited educational background and with little occupational need for legal service, working-class clients are apt to be less knowledgeable of law and lawyers than those from the middle and upper classes.

3. FEMALE CLIENTS It has been suggested that the dissolution of marriage in American society puts a greater burden on wives than husbands.[15] With the termination of marriage a woman exchanges her major adult status as a wife for the ambiguous status of the divorced or separated.[16] A change in a husband's marital status normally does not affect his primary status in the occupational structure. Viewed sociologically, then, a matrimonial action has greater consequences for women than men. It is significant that apart from emotionalism and ignorance the image most frequently ascribed to matrimonial cases refers to female clients. About one-fourth (27 per cent) of the sample reported that women are more difficult to represent than men in these cases.[17]

In discussing this attribute our informants talked about the greater emotionalism and ignorance of the law on the part of women clients. Nor was this merely a repetition of these two other images. Rather it implies an important social and psychological pattern in which individual characteristics are affected by social statuses: the extent to which clients manifest emotionalism and ignorance is determined partly by their status and roles as husband or wife. Both spouses may be upset and legally uninformed, but these attributes are more characteristic of wives than husbands. For example, the differential involvement of males and females in marriage conditions the psychological responses to a matrimonial action. Since the status of wife is more salient to women than the status of husband to men, the dissolution of marriage elicits different degrees of affect, as the informants recognized:

With some exceptions, women are far more difficult to deal with than men. They get so vindictive. They feel deprived, and the breakup is a much greater crisis for them and they just blow up.

Women are more emotional. Their lives are centered in the home. When the marriage breaks up, they are lost and resentful. I'm not talking about the executive female but the average woman.

The qualification in the last excerpt illustrates the structural dimension in the wife's situation. The "executive female" holds an important status outside of marriage which may enable her to sustain the loss of her position as wife with greater equanimity than the "average woman." Most American women, however, are probably "average" in the sense that they have no culturally important status equivalent to that of matrimony. Far more than husbands, wives are socially threatened by divorce or separation, and their emotional reactions are correspondingly more intense. As one informant expressed it: "The man's marriage may be on the rocks, he still has his job and things to look after. The woman has nothing, so she gets terribly upset and bitter."

The emotionalism of matrimonial clients, as we have seen, makes many lawyers uncomfortable because they find it difficult to cope with. Such clients are perceived as "hard to handle" and "difficult." We interpreted this perception as indicative of trained incapacity. Our interpretation seems to be substantiated by the image of a female client whose excessive emotionalism makes her a "more difficult" client than the male. One informant found women to be so emotional that he stopped accepting their cases. He explained: "Women are impossible to deal with. . . . They're bereft of logic and reason. I don't represent wives anymore." Avoidance is, of course, a well-known method of adjustment to a threatening situation. However, for many lawyers, it is an unrealistic one. For reasons described in Chapter 4, they are under pressure to accept matrimonial clients, male or female, even though the display of feminine emotion may leave them—as the next excerpt indicates —"at a loss," a phrase surely signifying trained incapacity:

Women get too emotional. They cry and carry on in here. When that happens, I keep wishing they were men. *I'm at a loss. What can I do?* The process of the law can't be explained to women when they act like that.

Client-ignorance, like emotionalism, is also related to differences between husband and wife statuses. In the course of their occupational careers husbands are more likely than wives to have some exposure to legal ideas and proceedings. As one lawyer noted, "Women, generally, haven't any experience with law and lawyers, and they have trouble understanding. Men are more likely to know what a lawyer can and cannot do." In short, matrimonial clients in general and wives in particular are characterized as being ignorant of law.

In discussing the female client, our informants raised another important factor that affects the lawyer-client relationship. In most types of legal actions, attorneys receive their fees from their clients. Matrimonial actions are an important exception: frequently, a husband is required to pay his wife's lawyer as well as his own. Normally, a wife is financially dependent on her husband who is bound by law to support her. When a marriage is dissolved, a husband may still be required to contribute to his ex-wife's support through the payment of alimony.[18] Until the adjudication of the decree, a considerable period of time may elapse during which the wife may have to support herself and hire an attorney. To meet this financial problem, the court has the power to grant, on motion of her lawyer, temporary alimony and counsel fees, pending litigation of the action. Alimony aside, this motion, if granted, requires that part of the wife's lawyer's fee be paid immediately by the husband; the remainder is paid when the action is put on the court's calendar. Under these conditions, attorneys may run a greater financial risk in representing wives rather than husbands. "If your client is a man," observed an informant, "he pays right away. With a woman client, where the money comes from the husband, it's harder." If husbands are reluctant to pay either the alimony or counsel fees, as many in New York County apparently are,[19] a lawyer can ask the court to punish him for contempt. This request, in many instances, is a futile gesture, as the next excerpt attests:

> Your fee usually comes from the husband, and if you represent the wife, you have to keep after him to get it. If he doesn't pay, you get a contempt motion. So you put him in jail, then he certainly can't pay. So you're licked before you start.[20]

The amount of a wife's counsel fees is determined by a judicial rule of thumb which ties these fees to the amount of alimony awarded. According to the informants, the court customarily allows wife's counsel a fee of ten times the weekly alimony. This procedure would seem to give lawyers a financial stake in negotiations over alimony. Actually, a husband's income and earn-ing power, his wife's age and occupational potential, the number and age of children, and other financially relevant variables impose limits on the size of the award. Nevertheless, in negotiations over a matrimonial action the wife's counsel fee can be used by either side as a bargaining point:

> Sometimes the husband's lawyer will immediately want to discuss your fee with you, figuring that if it is settled to your satisfaction, he'll be able to get concessions from you on other matters. . . . They're all positive that if the fee is settled they can deal with you.

The probability that an attorney will be asked to represent a wife depends on his type of practice. Wives will be relatively rare clients in business practices, more common among nonbusiness practices, and part of the daily routine in exclusively matrimonial practices. Our data provide tentative evidence that exposure to wife-clients is related to the reported difficulty in handling them. Lawyers with peripheral matrimonial practices were more likely than those with minor and major practices to cite the image of the female client; the ratio is expressed by the percentages 39:24:22.

The Matrimonial Problem

Two of the matrimonial images reported by lawyers referred to the nature of the client's problem: 23 per cent of the informants characterized matrimonial cases as *personal* problems, and 16 per cent described them as *nonlegal* problems.

The image of a personal problem is rooted in three conditions that lawyers encounter in these cases. First, the problem concerns clients in their private rather than their public statuses; it means a dispute arising out of their personal affairs and not, for example, out of their statuses as citizens, businessmen, voters, union members, tenants, or property owners. It is a problem involving, as one lawyer put it, "the intimate, personal lives of people." Second, as our previous discussion emphasized, the problem has emotional significance for the participants. To the clients, the issues in a matrimonial case are not trivial; they have a substantial emotional investment at stake. In the words of another lawyer: "They take their cases personally." Third, the disposition of a matrimonial action has important consequences for prevailing human relationships. "To win or lose in a matrimonial," noted an informant, "is to affect the lives of people."

Conversely, the absence of these conditions may result in legal problems being perceived as impersonal. Thus, one attorney described his "trade mark" cases as "too impersonal" and "lacking the personal touch." Similar sentiments were expressed by another lawyer in referring to "tax problems and real estate problems." "They're dry," he said, "and don't raise the kind of issues where people are directly involved." Clearly, people are involved in these so-called impersonal cases, but they are not clients in an individual capacity, nor do their problems directly concern and affect their private lives.

The definition of a legal problem as personal is not necessarily restricted to matrimonial cases. It could accurately apply to other kinds of cases, notably tort and criminal actions. In fact, it was so applied by several informants. Commented one: "In negligence and matrimonial work, you're dealing with the lives of people; it's very personal." And another pointed out that "in criminal work you're dealing with the lives of people."

Nevertheless, matrimonial cases still seem to possess a more personal quality than criminal or tort problems, which often have additional impersonal dimensions. Personal injury suits, for instance, generally pit stranger against stranger, and, more often than not, one of the two is an insurance company. Furthermore, the conflict often becomes a purely financial dispute. The personal nature of many criminal cases is diminished by two factors. First, the presence of government-employed, prosecuting attorneys tends to introduce an impersonal aspect to the proceedings. It is the state versus John Doe, not Doe versus Doe. Second, in many instances, defendants in criminal actions are perceived by lawyers as different from ordinary clients. This is particularly true where defendants have been involved in previous criminal cases. Such clients are frequently viewed not as individuals with personal problems, but as "people who are always in trouble," or as people "with a long record of convictions."

However personal a matrimonial case may be, it is still, after all, a legal problem. Why, then, is it characterized by some attorneys as nonlegal? The informants who reported this attribute were not denying the presence of legal issues in matrimonial actions; rather, they judged such issues to be incidental to the "real" problem, which was variously identified as "psychological," "social," and "medical."

This nonlegal orientation appears to be a product of the extremely personal quality of marital conflict, a quality that almost precludes its perception in legal terms. "Matrimonials," remarked one attorney, "involve the personal problems of people and really isn't a legal problem." In these cases, insisted another, "you're just wrapped up in the personal and emotional problems of people. It isn't really law." But why should a personal problem be perceived as not "really" law? Partly, because, in comparison to other types of legal problems, matrimonial cases do not require, in the opinion of some lawyers, the application of extensive legal knowledge. Said one: "From a legal point of view, you don't need to know much law." And another informant compared matrimonial actions with "real estate" cases where, in contrast, "you do have to use your legal knowledge to a great extent." "Marital cases are not hard in terms of knowing law," observed a third informant, "nothing like my commercial practice." The belief that matrimonial problems demand little in the way of legal skill is reinforced by the correlative awareness that other kinds of skills are more appropriate:

The matrimonials don't require talent, *not legal talent. You have to understand human nature.*

The legal work isn't difficult. It's ironing all the emotional problems out. It's the time and patience required.

In brief, since a matrimonial case is defined as putting a minimum on legal skill and a premium on nonlegal knowledge, it evokes an image of a legal problem that is not "really" legal.

Again, the influence of type of practice on professional imagery can be seen in the different proportions of lawyers referring to personal and nonlegal problems. Attorneys with peripheral matrimonial practices, that is, those who normally serve business clients, were much more likely to define marital cases as personal than were those with major practices; 39 per cent of the former and 17 per cent of the latter cited this image. For the peripheral practitioner, a separation or divorce action represents a distinct departure from more impersonal commercial and corporation work. For the major practitioner, the constant repetition of matrimonial cases apparently makes the image less salient. With reference to the nonlegal image, the pattern is reversed: 11 per cent of those with peripheral practices and 22 per cent of those with major practices referred to it. It would seem that an awareness of the inappropriateness of legal knowledge depends on the scope of a lawyer's matrimonial practice.

Effects of Matrimonial Cases on Lawyers

A norm common to all professions admonishes practitioners to remain objective toward the problems brought to them by laymen. It is assumed that if a professional loses his objectivity, if he gets personally involved, he is less able to help his client.[21] The importance of the norm in law practice is implied in an old aphorism: "A lawyer who represents himself has a fool for a client." Among the images reported by our informants was one referring to the personal involvement of attorneys in matrimonial cases. Although the necessity of remaining objective was readily acknowledged, 17 per cent of the sample admitted that it was difficult to do so in these cases. For example:

It's very hard to stay detached in a matrimonial, yet you should.

You have to stay out, keep your feelings out of marital cases. Sometimes that is impossible. Slowly you find yourself completely involved emotionally, even when you are trying not to.

The problem of involvement does not appear to impinge with equal frequency in all types of practice. The ratio of those citing it varied by type of matrimonial practice: from one out of three with major practices, to about one out of five with peripheral practices, to about one out of ten with minor practices. However, it is the *content* of the image, as much as its variation, that is significant. In discussing involvement, lawyers with major matrimonial practices never referred to themselves but always to the involvement of attorneys who did less matrimonial work; minor and peripheral practitioners, on the other hand, talked about their own tendency to become involved. The consensus seems to be that involvement in marital cases is primarily a problem for lawyers who do not have extensive matrimonial practices. Moreover, slightly more than half of the informants in the latter category also indicated that the problem was greater in matrimonial than in other kinds of legal work. "Lawyers are more apt to get involved in marital than in other types of cases," said one of them.

Because most attorneys do not have major matrimonial practices, the problem of involvement is probably fairly common in law practice. It becomes important, therefore, to look more closely at the pressures that inhibit or facilitate loss of professional detachment in these cases. Our analysis reveals at least seven relevant variables:

1. PRESSURE FROM THE CLIENT Matrimonial clients, as we reported, want lawyers to share their feelings. They explicitly invite counsel's involvement. If this invitation is accepted, professional detachment is plainly reduced. The penalty paid by lawyers who comply with their clients' wishes was noted by an informant:

> These people are all aroused, and they want you, the lawyer, to be as aroused as they are. . . . *If a lawyer starts getting involved like that, he loses whatever effectiveness he may have.*

2. Violation of Cultural Norms Even should a client not attempt to involve him, the substance of a particular matrimonial case might elicit a highly affective response from a lawyer and lessen his objectivity. More specifically, the alleged facts in an action may pertain to violations of deeply ingrained cultural norms, violations that may evoke a nonprofessional reaction in an attorney. And this may occur, as the next excerpt states, despite an attorney's effort to control his response:

A matrimonial client comes in and tells her story. . . . Say it is a sad story, and perhaps revolting, maybe even involving degeneracy. Well, *the lawyer must react as a human being*. He may feel that we'll teach the other side a lesson. *Now I deplore this feeling and guard against it in myself. But it happens.*

3. Female Clients According to our informants, lawyers are more apt to become involved with a female than a male client. This is probably due, in part, to the greater emotional demands made by many women clients. But there is another contributing factor: most lawyers are males, and many female matrimonial clients reportedly turn to their male lawyers for the general advice and sympathy that they previously obtained from their spouses. "The woman client," said one attorney, "will tend to rely on the lawyer. He becomes a kind of substitute husband. You feel sorry and don't want to hurt her." Thus, given the intensely emotional context of these actions and its differential effect on men and women, female clients often invest considerable affect in their relationship with male counsel. Under these circumstances, as an informant pointed out, "it can be tough not to get involved." The same informant went on to say:

The woman in many cases hasn't anyone else to talk to. The husband may have been the only man in her life, even though he was no good. You are her defender. She is grateful, lonely, and, if you are lucky, she's ugly.

4. FRIENDS AND STRANGERS In some matrimonial cases, lawyers represent their relatives, friends, or acquaintances; in others, the clients are strangers. A lawyer, it appears, is less likely to lose his objectivity if he has no other relationship to a client except the professional one. Conversely, in representing a friend or relative, the accumulated sentiments of nonprofessional attachments can lessen an attorney's detached concern, as the next excerpt illustrates:

Many of my matrimonial clients are the children of my regular clients. . . . I've watched them grow up. I get personally involved and it's very difficult. Sometimes I get to the point where I can't take it, and I get out of the case.

5. LAWYERS' FAMILIAL STATUSES After commenting on the problem he faced in remaining objective in these cases, an attorney drew our attention to another relevant variable with this remark: "If the lawyer is married, with children of his own, it is harder yet." The implied hypothesis is clear: insofar as a matrimonial case deals with personal relationships common to the lawyer and his client, it becomes more difficult for him to stay detached.* A client's problem may strike harmonic or discordant overtones in an attorney's private life and provide a ready basis for identification. In describing how he helped a husband-client obtain custody of the client's child, one lawyer had this to say:

* Eight lawyers in the sample had been divorced or separated. According to all of them, the experience of personally participating in a matrimonial action made them neither more nor less likely to become involved with their matrimonial clients.

I was determined myself to get that youngster away from that woman. . . . *I thought of my own child.* And I guess one reason I was so interested was that *my girl was exactly the same age as my client's girl. And I thought what if my girl had to live with a woman like that.* Well, we finally won, and *it was quite a thrill for me* to see that girl back with her father.

6. WORKING ON THE CASE We noted before how some of the legally required steps in a New York matrimonial action often increase client-emotionalism. In a similar fashion, by simply working on the necessary details of his client's problem, by striving to find a solution to a marital dispute, a lawyer may slowly find himself losing detachment. When the number and complexity of personal issues increase, as they do when children are involved, the pattern of involvement through work becomes more manifest:

I mean after you hear all the facts and work out the future of the children, their schooling, and all the intimate details of their lives, it becomes hard—I'd say impossible—to remain detached. After a while it becomes a crusade for you.

7. DETACHMENT THROUGH EXPERIENCE Finally, as we pointed out, the number of matrimonial cases handled by a lawyer appears to influence his susceptibility to involvement. Said one matrimonial specialist: "If you have a lawyer who is inexperienced in matrimonials, he gets all involved." To which we may add the complementary observation made by a general practitioner: "The matrimonial specialist, or the one who has handled quite a few of them, keeps pretty detached."

In their descriptions of matrimonial cases, our informants frequently used words that indicated their own sense of frustration, words that support our earlier judgment of trained incapacity. The impact of these cases on counsel was described as "exhausting," "devastating," "depressing," "trying," and "demanding," to choose but a handful of examples. As these terms plainly imply, a matrimonial action can subject a lawyer to a substantial degree of stress. In the words of one informant, "It can be too emotional and wearing on you." This attribute of strain, the psychological wear and tear experienced by counsel, was cited by 28 per cent of the sample.[22]

Almost every attorney who mentioned the image of strain also noted that it grew out of the extensive time required to reassure emotional clients. These clients, we were informed, tend to be so anxious that a lawyer "has to lead them by the hand, humor them, be mother and father to them, and listen, listen, listen." Supportive behavior of this type may comfort a client but it exacts an emotional toll from a lawyer:

> You have to take a lot of guff listening to these people, and you must learn to take it without showing it, or getting tired, or retaliating.

The strain induced by time-consuming efforts to provide psychological support to distraught clients is accentuated by the reported persistency of clients who demand not just reassurance, but constant reassurance. Matrimonial clients were pictured by lawyers as people who "are always calling you"; who "won't leave you alone"; who "are always coming by the office or want you to come by their place"; who "call you all the time and it doesn't make any difference whether you are in the office or at home." The informants complained of three aspects of this persistency: (a) it interferes with work for other clients; (b) matrimonial clients are seeking additional personal support, not further legal advice; and (c) it represents a service for which there is no adequate compensation. Or, as one attorney summarized them:

Marital clients act as if the lawyer has nothing else to do but listen to them. And most of the time, it is not about some legal issue. They just want to talk to someone who is on their side. . . . You can never charge them enough for all the work and headaches.

Unlike those with peripheral or minor practices, lawyers who concentrate or specialize in matrimonial cases are constantly exposed to the supportive demands of these clients. The difference in practice and exposure is revealed in the saliency of the image: the attribute of strain was cited by more than half of the major practitioners (56 per cent) but only about one out of five other lawyers referred to it. We cannot infer from this that specialists experience more stress than nonspecialists; but it is plausible to assume that the specialists are more aware of the stress and, perhaps, better adjusted to it. "It's nerve-wracking work," admitted one specialist, "but you get used to it."

Although they may "get used to it," major matrimonial practitioners must constantly deal with the demands of their clients. They are, as one of them put it, "like obstetricians . . . on call all the time." This "on call" feature suggests that matrimonial practices require more direct personal supervision by lawyers than other kinds of practice. As one specialist explained:

Generally speaking, I like the type of work I do. But it's exhausting, and I sometimes wish I were in corporation law or surrogate practice. *This kind of practice requires your constant attention.* If I were in corporation or probate work, I could make a date for golf and know that I could keep it. Or I could take a vacation and really forget the office. When I go on vacation, I call the office every day.

The strain experienced by lawyers with peripheral matrimonial practices takes a different form. These attorneys usually have fewer marital clients than other lawyers; they are less exposed to the emotional demands of such clients. However, the few matrimonial cases they handle generally involve individuals already known to them. This added personal context, which does not prevail in other types of practice, can compound the stress associated with these cases. An informant with a commercial practice had this to say about the problem:

> Say one of your regular clients discovered his wife in adultery and wants a divorce. Well, she's your friend, too, and it becomes very embarrassing and difficult. In fact, most of our marital cases come from relatives or friends of our regular clients. It creates a real strain.

It is, of course, true that all types of legal cases put some degree of strain on lawyers. Until we have comparative data on the kinds and degrees of stress generated by different types of cases, we can only speculate on the meaning of this attribute in matrimonial practice. Our provisional judgment is this: Since most lawyers are not professionally trained to cope with the characteristic emotionalism of matrimonial clients, dealing with these clients will subject them to more strain than cases where their skills are more relevant. Consequently, behavior that psychiatrists and social workers take in their stride will continue to disconcert members of the legal profession. The reported image of strain lends support to this interpretation.

Additional evidence supporting this judgment is found in the principal explanation for the fact that some attorneys refuse to accept matrimonial cases: namely, that many lawyers do not care to experience the emotional strain imposed by these cases on counsel and, therefore, reject them as a matter of policy.[23] Of fifty-six informants—slightly more than two-thirds of the sample—who personally knew such attorneys, 40 per cent gave this explanation.

Lawyers' Attitudes toward Matrimonial Cases

Our review of professional imagery has provided some knowledge of the ways in which the lawyer-client relationship is affected by attributes of matrimonial cases. We have yet to consider the professional attitudes toward these cases. We asked the informants whether they liked or disliked handling matrimonial actions. A plurality of 39 per cent expressed a liking for the cases, 35 per cent said they were indifferent, and 26 per cent expressed dislike.

When these attitudes are examined by type of matrimonial practice, different patterns appear. Almost all of the major practitioners (94 per cent) stated a preference for these cases, most minor practitioners (56 per cent) were indifferent, and most peripheral practitioners (78 per cent) disliked them.

In accounting for their attitudes most attorneys pointed to one or more components of their professional images. About two-thirds of those who liked the cases explained their preference in terms of the gratification they received from (a) helping people in general (b) and helping them with personal problems in particular. Although these reasons were given by minor and major practitioners, one-third of the latter also based their preference on the fact that their professional reputations were identified with matrimonial cases. The reasons most frequently cited by lawyers who disliked the cases were (a) the strain imposed on counsel, (b) inadequate compensation, and (c) the personal nature of matrimonial problems. The informants who said they were indifferent to these cases indicated that they viewed the cases as an accepted part of law practice, and, as such, they neither liked nor disliked them. Appropriately, most of the indifferent attorneys had minor practices in which they were neither completely dependent on the cases, nor were required to take them as a service to regular clients.

THE LAWYER'S ROLE IN MATRIMONIAL ACTIONS

CHAPTER 6

The professional imagery of matrimonial cases, as we have just seen, provides some important clues concerning the effects of these cases on the lawyer-client relationship. We now need to consider lawyers' conceptions of their professional role in marital actions.

We can anticipate that our informants' role definitions will vary with their patterns of law practice. However, if it is true that professional behavior is influenced by the structure of practice, it does not follow necessarily that lawyers with similar practices will handle the same type of case in the same way; they may hold different conceptions about the general nature of a lawyer's job, and, consequently, behave differently. Therefore, before presenting our informants' specific role definitions, we shall examine their broad conceptions of a lawyer's role.

Role Orientations

The role of a lawyer consists of the behavior that the courts, bar associations, and clients expect of him by virtue of his occupying the lawyer status. But people engaged in the same role activity assign different meanings to that activity; they have various conceptions about what the role is, what it should be, and what it might become. The meanings that lawyers assign to their professional work may be called their role orientations.[1]

There is enough available evidence to suggest that variation in role orientation has important behavioral consequences. For example, in one study,[2] the receptivity of a sample of physicians to a new drug was shown to be related to two distinct orientations: doctors who were oriented primarily to the medical profession adopted the drug more quickly than those oriented primarily to their patients. And, in another study,[3] a relationship was found between accuracy in writing newspaper stories and journalists' orientations: the accuracy with which journalists wrote "good" and "bad" news varied with their orientation to imagined readers. These, and similar, findings [4] emphasize the importance of role orientation in shaping professional role performance.

To classify our informants by role orientation, we analyzed their responses to questions about satisfaction and frustration in law practice.[5] These questions were asked prior to any discussion about matrimonial cases.

Our analysis produced three major role orientations: orientations toward problems, people, and money.

1. Problem-Oriented Lawyers Thirty-six attorneys were classified as having problem orientations. These informants look for and obtain primary satisfaction through the successful applications of their skills and knowledge to the solution of problems arising in law practice. Although they appear to share an image of the lawyer as a problem-solver, their sources of gratification and sense of accomplishment derive from different kinds of problems.

a. *The Trial Lawyer.* The most challenging problems in the practice of law are to be found, for some lawyers, in trial work. For these attorneys, legal problems become gratifying when they result in litigation: "No matter what type of case, if it gets to a trial, I enjoy it." To a trial-oriented lawyer, meeting the problems of a trial is the capstone of professional endeavor:

The lawyer at his finest, in my opinion, is found in trial work.

A good trial is, for me, the real lawyer's work.

There are several qualities about the problems attending courtroom litigation that appeal to lawyers with this orientation. First, they enjoy the controversy: "I like the idea of a contest, of fighting to win." Second, the battle-of-wits that such work often entails appeals to them: "I love trying to outmaneuver, outfight, outsmart the other side." Third, they view the ability to be persuasive as an index of professional talent: "You have to present your side to a jury, twelve people with their own problems. You have to convince them. You have to know your stuff and how to present it." Finally, the public nature of a trial is a source of gratification; the service a lawyer renders to his client is highly visible: "It's dramatic and I like being in the limelight. The client can see you fight and he knows that he is in your hands." With their strong orientation to trials, these lawyers get small satisfaction from the non-litigious aspects of practice, aspects which they tend to view as "routine" and "boring," and which they are apt to disparage. Said one: "The rest of law practice—office work, research, writing briefs—it all seems to be stringing words together . . . quibbling over what a word does, or does not, mean."

b. *The Technician.* The technician is oriented in his role toward research and analysis. He sees himself as a highly skilled expert exploring the ins and outs of complex puzzles. He is interested in problems that have little saliency for trial-oriented lawyers. As the following excerpts illustrate, the content of a legal problem may vary, but if it is perceived as complex, its solution becomes a primary source of gratification:

I like to work on a knotty, interesting problem, one which may involve a good deal of research. The more technical it is, the better.

I like legal problems to be involved or complicated, where you have to study the matter carefully, where you may have to write a careful brief.

The work I enjoy the most is . . . perpetuity and trust. There are problems in that work which are just fascinating. It's unravelling the problem that I find so interesting. I love complicated problems which have to be solved.

A complicated legal problem to the technician seems to be one in which, first, there is no immediately obvious solution; second, he must take time to study it carefully; and, third, considerable research is required. His approach to problems tends to be intellectual, if not scholarly. Given this orientation, the technician is apt to dislike legal work that does not require considered thought and analysis; to him, such work appears "routine" or "mechanical." He also tends to dislike trial work, not because it is considered easy, but because it elicits professional behavior that conflicts with his role orientation. Trials, in his judgment, do not allow counsel enough time to analyze problems, and they require skills which he does not evaluate very highly. One technician explained his dislike of the trial work associated with criminal and negligence cases:

There is very little research in either of them. It's mostly a matter of being able to handle yourself in court. Lawyers who specialize in these two areas are courtroom technicians only. They're good at courtroom examination and dealing with juries and judges. I prefer cases where you have time to think through a complex problem.

c. *The Business Organizer.* The organizer is oriented mainly toward solving problems related to business organization. His chief gratification in practice comes not from participation in trials or solving difficult legal problems but from establishing or reorganizing business enterprises. For this type of lawyer, problem-solving is affectively related to his ability to establish or maintain, in cooperation with others, an operating and observable organization. Commented one organizer: "I enjoy setting businesses up, solving problems, and getting things so well organized that the business can function. Seeing the business established is the thing." This orientation was expressed by another informant who described his most satisfying law work as "work which calls for conferences between men which result in mergers; where you bring together groups of men and talent and see something grow out of the meetings."

Of our thirty-six problem-oriented informants, seventeen were oriented as trial lawyers, fifteen as technicians, and four as business organizers. Conspicuously absent from these orientations is any significant reference to clients. Indeed, going over these interviews, we get the impression that clients are almost inconsequential to these attorneys as long as they have an opportunity to sink their teeth into problems.

2. People-Oriented Lawyers Twenty lawyers in our sample were classified as having an orientation toward people. Their descriptions of professional gratification were stated primarily in terms of the satisfaction received from interpersonal relationships. They like cases where "the development of human relations is paramount," where "people are directly involved." Problems, to these lawyers, mean people; and they emphasize the image of a lawyer as a helper. Said one: "After all, what is a lawyer? Someone who helps people."

The orientation toward people has five distinguishing characteristics. First, it is an orientation that focuses on clients in their individual and not representative statuses; the clients are served as persons, not as members of groups or organizations.

Second, these clients become a particular source of gratification to lawyers if they are perceived as "ordinary," if they do not differ in any significant way from most normal individuals. "I represent," noted one informant, "mostly ordinary people, not great business affairs. I get great personal pleasure out of helping small people with their problems." This sentiment does not mean that these attorneys dislike handling the problems of wealthy or famous clients. It does suggest, however, that working with "ordinary" individuals can be rewarding partly because they have no special claim to deference. It seems as though, in some instances, a lawyer's professional self-esteem depends on serving those who cannot readily command service, and whose relative helplessness enhances his work. But this form of psychic income is not obtained if the client is perceived as a deviant. Thus, people-oriented lawyers dislike most criminal cases because the clients are "hardened criminals." Criminal cases are acceptable if they are about, what one attorney called, "clean crime"; that is, where an otherwise law-abiding citizen is charged with crime:

> I don't mind taking a criminal case where I know the alleged crime may be accidental or a once-in-a-lifetime thing. Two men may get angry and in their passion fight and one may kill the other. They aren't criminals the way hardened criminals are criminal. I dislike representing a person with a long record of past convictions. I don't feel comfortable and I avoid the situation.

Third, strong emphasis is put on *helping* clients. Cases are satisfying where "you feel that you are helping clients with their worries and problems," cases "where people can't help themselves," and where an attorney feels that he is "doing something for someone." This source of gratification assumes, of course, that there is an available solution to a client's problem. Under conditions where there is no legal recourse, the lawyer assesses the situation as one in which he is helpless as a lawyer. Such conditions were often associated with criminal cases by the people-oriented lawyers; specifically, the "hardened criminal" was defined as a client whom a lawyer could not help: "Where I'm asked to defend a hardened criminal, I feel that there is no hope for this guy. He's not going to change. If I get him off, he'll be back in trouble. . . . I don't like that kind of case. *I don't feel that I'm doing anything.*" Similarly, another lawyer commented: "You can see how and why criminals stay that way. It bothers me. *What can you do with them?"* Probably all lawyers feel somewhat uncomfortable when they cannot help their clients, but an orientation to helping people makes the sense of discomfort especially acute.

Fourth, people-oriented lawyers conceive of their services in strongly personal terms. As the following excerpts illustrate, they visualize themselves as actively intervening in their clients' personal lives:

> I find the immigration work the most satisfying type of work. . . . *The adjustment of the lives of people who desire to be decent citizens* is very satisfying.
>
> I would say, in general, that to be able to *straighten people's lives out in matrimonial problems* gives me a lot of satisfaction.
>
> I enjoy cases . . . where I'm dealing with some poor individual caught in a problem. . . . For example, I've done a good deal of military work *where I get bad* [*conduct*] *discharges changed into honorable ones. . . . I personally prefer such personal cases.*

Help that is not perceived as personal does not provide much gratification to these lawyers. An informant who indicated his preference for negligence and matrimonial cases "because of the human beings involved," went on to add: "I've done a lot of commercial work and don't care for it. It's too impersonal; no human relationships are at stake." Similar sentiments were expressed by another informant who disliked "real estate closings" because they "don't raise the kind of issue where you can see the effect in the lives of people."

Fifth, in providing personal help, these lawyers are not only oriented toward affecting their clients' lives, they also desire, as was just noted, "to *see* the effect" of their efforts—a concern with visible consequences of professional work. This sensitivity to visibility is similar, but not identical, to that found in two of the problem orientations. The trial lawyer seems mainly interested in the public observability of his work in progress; he is seen performing his role. The business organizer, on the other hand, seems more interested in an observable product, a functioning business enterprise. In contrast to both of these, the people-oriented attorney appears to be principally concerned with visible alterations in his clients' personal lives.

3. *Money-Oriented Lawyers* Thirteen of our informants emphasized the importance of financial reward in their descriptions of work satisfaction. To them, a case is not primarily an opportunity to solve problems or to help clients, but a chance to earn a fee. "All legal work is satisfying," said one, "I get paid for it." We may assume that income is important to all lawyers but, as the next array of excerpts indicates, these informants seem to give it greater priority than those with other orientations:

To be honest, the work that is the most lucrative is the most satisfying.

I like real estate cases because the fees are pretty good. I dislike commercial work; it involves a lot of work for very little money.

If you want the truth, I prefer the kind of work that pays me the most with the least amount of work.

The references to honesty in these excerpts may mean that our money-oriented lawyers were more candid in their responses than other attorneys who may have been reluctant to admit a primary concern with legal fees. Granted that such a reluctance may have influenced the responses of some informants, nevertheless there are reasons for believing that a major interest in monetary reward is but one of several distinctive occupational orientations. (1) There is evidence that economic rewards are not necessarily the principal source of gratification for members of various occupations.[6] (2) Some of our problem- and people-oriented informants often said they enjoyed receiving a large fee, but they also pointed out that the fee, in itself, did not give them as much satisfaction as solving problems or helping people. Some of them further observed that the most gratifying aspects of practice were frequently the least lucrative. (3) A few informants who expressed some dissatisfaction with their income reported that they had turned down opportunities to increase their incomes by joining business companies; given a chance to make more money, they chose to remain in independent, and presumably, more gratifying law practice.

Our data suggest that the role orientations that we have described may well be derived from anticipatory images of work which motivated our informants to enter the legal profession. A few interview comments seem to point to this conclusion:

> For awhile as a young man I was on the fence about a career. I couldn't make up my mind between law and business. . . . In some ways I'm a frustrated business executive. So I get a good deal of satisfaction out of problems of business organization and reorganization.

> I love trial work. . . . I think that it represents the traditional view of the lawyer as an advocate. It was that picture of the lawyer that brought me into law.

> When I was a young man I wanted to be a minister, then a social worker, then a lawyer. . . . Then I went to law school. I've been helping people ever since.

More systematic evidence bearing on the relationship between present role orientation and earlier, preprofessional orientation is found in Rosenberg's study of undergraduates' occupational values. Among a large sample of college students he discovered three major value complexes representing types of gratification toward which students were oriented. These clusters of values bear a close resemblance to the role orientations reported by our informants. Rosenberg describes those adhering to a "people-oriented value complex" as individuals who "tend to view work largely as an opportunity for obtaining the gratification to be derived from interpersonal relations." This appears to be an accurate description of the people-oriented lawyer. His description of individuals oriented to an "extrinsic-reward" complex fits our characterization of the money-oriented lawyer: those who "tend to emphasize the reward to be obtained *for* work, rather than the gratifications to be derived *from* work." Finally, he classifies people whose value complex is oriented to "self-expression" as individuals who "tend to view work chiefly as an end in itself, as an opportunity for expressing their talent and creative potentialities." This seems to be an apt description of the problem-oriented lawyer. Furthermore, his findings show that all three of these value complexes were important to students who were planning to choose law as a career. They had higher than average scores in the "people-oriented" and "external-reward" complexes and slightly under the average in the "self-expression" complex; in no value area did they have extremely low or high scores.[7]

An attorney's role orientation represents, to some degree, his self-image imposed on his conception of professional work; it is the subjective meaning he assigns to the role of a lawyer. But role orientations are not idiosyncratic. Although they vary in content, they are shared by others. Do, then, lawyers with the same orientations have other characteristics in common? The size and nature of our sample prevent us from answering the question in an adequate manner. Yet we did look for clues by cross-tabulating lawyers' role orientations by other attributes. The results appear in Table 3. There

Table 3: Role Orientations by Attributes of Law Practice, in Per Cent [a]

ATTRIBUTES OF LAW PRACTICE	*ROLE ORIENTATIONS*			
	Problem	*People*	*Money*	*Number in Group* [b]
Lawyers' fathers' occupations				
Professional and business executive	64	18	18	(17)
Small business and "white collar"	47	36	17	(36)
Skilled and unskilled labor	50	25	25	(16)
Type of law school attended				
University	70	20	10	(20)
Catholic	37	44	19	(16)
Independent	49	27	24	(33)
Organization of practice				
Solo	37	34	29	(38)
Partnership	71	23	6	(31)
Types of cases [c]				
General	52	20	28	(25)
Personal service	29	64	7	(14)
Business	59	18	23	(22)
Clients' class background				
Upper	69	23	8	(13)
Middle	55	27	18	(22)
Working	44	32	24	(34)
Types of matrimonial practice				
Peripheral	69	25	6	(16)
Minor	45	25	30	(40)
Major	53	47	—	(13)

[a] Per cents are added horizontally.

[b] Excludes thirteen lawyers who could not be classified by role orientation.

[c] Excludes eight lawyers with specialties in both personal service and business cases.

appears to be a fairly distinct association of characteristics among those with a problem orientation, and less distinct patterns for those oriented toward people and money. The data suggest that problem-oriented lawyers are more apt than others to have relatively high class origins, to have attended a university law school, to practice in partnership, to have fairly affluent clients, and to engage in peripheral matrimonial practices. People-oriented attorneys are more likely to come from middle- and working-class backgrounds, to have attended Catholic and independent law schools, and to have personal service practices, often concentrating in matrimonial law. Money-oriented lawyers are apt to have a working-class background, to have gone to an independent law school, to be solo general practitioners, to have a working-class clientele, and minor matrimonial practices.

Do these role orientations change during a lawyer's career? To answer this query properly, we would have to examine the same attorneys at different stages in their careers. Nevertheless, it is worth noting that the length of time in practice does not substantially change the distribution of these orientations. Among those informants who were in practice for nineteen years or less, the proportions oriented toward problems, people, and money are 52, 29, and 19 per cent, respectively; among those in practice for twenty years or more, the respective percentages are 55, 29, and 16.

As we might anticipate, role orientations affect an attorney's attitude toward matrimonial cases. Characteristically, people-oriented attorneys find an opportunity in matrimonial actions to obtain satisfaction from helping their clients with personal problems. Of those oriented toward people, 70 per cent claimed that they liked these cases. For most problem-oriented lawyers, the same kind of case represents "too much emotion," too few problems, and considerable strain. Among the problem-oriented informants, 28 per cent expressed a preference for the cases, 36 per cent were indifferent, and 36 per cent disliked them. Concerned primarily with financial rewards, most money-oriented lawyers (69 per cent) expressed an indifferent attitude; only 8 per cent preferred this kind of case while 23 per cent did not.

Role Definitions

In our examination of role orientations we found that law practice, like other kinds of professional work, has diverse meanings for different practitioners. We turn now to a related question: How do professionals describe their role when they are confronted with a specific type of problem? More concretely, what are lawyers' definitions of their role in matrimonial cases?

The analysis in this section is based on our informants' responses to a direct query: "As you see it, what is the lawyer's basic job when he represents a matrimonial client?" Four lawyers gave answers that were either too vague or ambiguous for classification; five said that reconciliation was the lawyer's basic job. The answers provided by seventy-three attorneys were classified into two major role definitions: one is labeled the Counselor's role; the other, the Advocate's role.

1. THE COUNSELOR As defined by forty-seven informants, the job of an attorney in a matrimonial case is primarily to ascertain the nature of the client's problem and then to work toward a solution that is fair to both spouses. This role definition emphasizes the active part played by a lawyer in his relationship with a client. The Counselor participates in three important ways.

First, he attempts to clarify, to his own satisfaction, the content of his client's problem. He tends not to accept at face value the client's version of marital difficulties; instead, he looks for what he considers to be the underlying problem:

> You try and get a feeling for what's underneath. What's the real story? I don't put it to clients that way, but that's what I'm after.

The value of being able to identify the underlying problem, or "real story," is that it enables the Counselor to arrive at an independent diagnosis of the client's case, which, in turn, permits him to distinguish between the client's opinion and his own professional judgment. As one informant explained: "Clients may come in here and tell you what they want when I know that is not what they need. . . . You keep listening and questioning until you feel that pang [sic], that pang that tells you what's underneath. . . . She may want a divorce but what she needs is a separation. You have to keep in mind the distinction between the two."

Second, the Counselor attempts to discover what, in his opinion, would be the most beneficial solution for the client. As our informants so often expressed it: "You try and figure out what is best for the client." This, too, requires an independent judgment in which the lawyer weighs his view against the client's. He asks himself, in the words of one attorney, "Will the action which the client contemplates help her?"

Finally, the Counselor participates in an effort to work out a solution to the problem that is also fair to the opposing spouse: "We try for the best solution for all concerned." This interest in a reasonably fair solution grows out of the lawyer's concern for his client who he feels is best served through reasonable negotiation and settlement. Unfair solutions, particularly where the opposing side is forced to yield excessively, may gratify his client, but the Counselor dislikes them because they eventually raise further problems that could be avoided. Here is one informant's explanation of this point:

Suppose I get a huge alimony for a wife and I know that it is more than the man can afford in terms of spendable income. Well the wife thinks it's wonderful and I'm a great lawyer in her eyes. But in a few years he won't pay it any more; he can't afford it. He was anxious to get divorced and wasn't too cautious, but now it is impossible. Maybe he wants to re-marry. He's angry. He can't pay. The situation deteriorates. Why? Because the contract was not feasible to begin with. . . . I try for fairness in such situations, a settlement which can serve as a guide for my client for a long time.

The Counselor's goal of a fair solution is sustained by his disinclination to make extreme demands of the opposition. He wants his side to prevail but with qualifications: "I do the best job I can for my client within certain limits. The limits are these: If the husband is my client, I do not believe in cutting off the wife without a cent; if I represent the wife, I do not believe in taking the husband for every cent he's got. . . . Generally I try for a fair settlement, and within these limits I try and win the case."

2. THE ADVOCATE As defined by twenty-six of our informants, the major task of a lawyer in a matrimonial case is to achieve the results desired by the client. This role definition emphasizes the relatively passive part played by a lawyer in his relationship with clients. As the next array of excerpts implies, the definition of the problem and its solution are made primarily by the client, not the lawyer:

I try and accomplish the purpose that the client has in mind.

The lawyer's job is to get the client the results they want. Whatever they want I get for them provided it's not illegal and can be done.

My first job is to carry out their wishes.

If the Counselor takes the client's statement of intent as a point of departure for his own independent analysis, the Advocate takes it as a cue for action. The latter proceeds on the assumption that the client's plans are clear and certain: "I simply get them results. . . . They know what they want to do, so I simply carry out their desires. I work out the details." In centering his role definition around the client's will, the Advocate tends, correlatively, to give less weight to his own judgment. "Our job," observed one, "is to do what the client wants regardless of what we think or feel."

In performing his role the Advocate is guided by one general principle: within the limits of the law, he seeks maximum benefits for his client. He tries, as one attorney noted, "to do the most" and "get away with what you can for that client." Or, as another lawyer expressed it: "I tell you my job is to do the best thing for my client, that is, to get the best deal for my client."

The content of a "best deal" varies from case to case. However, the Advocate is apt to perceive it mainly as an economic issue; his specific goal then varies with the client's sex:

In matrimonial cases clients are primarily interested in money. If you represent the wife, then your job is to get as much as possible for her. If you represent the husband, pay out as little as possible.

Success in a matrimonial action is defined by the Advocate as the triumph of his client over his opponent.

In or out of court, he is oriented toward eventual victory. He is out "to win," to "beat the other fellow." Where he is able, in the name of the client, to defeat the opposing spouse decisively, he is apt to feel a strong sense of professional accomplishment. One informant described his recent achievements: "I might say that we have a small reputation for being pretty good at this stuff. We have recently had amazing success defending husbands. We had seven or eight cases in a row where the woman got zero. You have to assume that the judge will lean over backwards to be fair to a woman, so when you win the way we do, it's quite a thing."

Furthermore, in striving to attain client-defined objectives, the Advocate tends to feel that he is demonstrating his ability to the client and that this is necessary. If the Counselor seems to take his professional skills for granted, the Advocate does not, as the next excerpt illustrates:

What's fair support? . . . Let's say, on the basis of the man's income . . . the courts have been going along with something between twenty and thirty dollars a week for support. . . . Now the opposing lawyer tells me that the wife wants, or will settle for, twenty-five dollars a week for the children. Now my client can afford twenty-five dollars and probably would go along with it. But he figures that his wife will get part of that for herself, and, besides, he's going to buy clothes, toys, and take the children out. So he hedges a bit. Then he figures, *well, what have I, his lawyer, done for him?* He could have accepted that without a lawyer. So I tell him that legally that is a reasonable solution, but I'll see what I can do. I tell the other lawyer that my client wants to pay twenty dollars. So we dicker back and forth. Finally, we agree on twenty-two-fifty a week. I tell the husband and he agrees, and we end on that. *You have to show the client that you are doing something for him.*

Two observations need to be made about these role definitions. First, the Advocate's role appears to be much more clearly defined than the Counselor's. Reading their interviews, we get the impression that Advocates view their relationship with marital clients in a rather simple, straightforward—almost mechanical—manner. They seem to have a "tell-me-what-you-want-and-I'll-see-if-I-can-get-it" attitude. In contrast, the Counselor's role appears less structured, more flexible, even ambiguous. In emphasizing his own judgment rather than the client's, he is willing to consider dimensions other than those presented by clients in defining and solving problems. Second, it should be kept in mind that these role definitions are not mutually exclusive; each gives priority to different aspects of professional behavior. The Counselor undoubtedly engages in some advocacy, and the Advocate surely does some counseling. The significant finding is that lawyers differ in the degree to which they define their tasks as approximating one role or the other.

Counselors and Advocates not only have different interpretations of a lawyer's role in a matrimonial case; they also differ in their attitudes toward clients' presentation of facts, the extent to which they attempt to influence clients' decisions, and their complaints about clients' misbehavior.

We reported, in Chapter 2, our informants' opinion that parties to New York matrimonial actions frequently deceive the court through fraud, collusion, and connivance. This they generally blamed on the legal system. However, it has been suggested that lawyers themselves play no small part in encouraging such deceit.[8] We have no data bearing on this charge, but we did query our informants about their reactions to a client's version of the facts concerning matrimonial conflict. Our question was: "How can a lawyer be sure that his client's story is accurate?"

The replies tended to reflect the reported role definitions. A greater proportion of Advocates than Counselors took the position that an attorney must assume that his client's story is true; 38 per cent of the former and 15 per cent of the latter expressed this view. Said one Advocate: "A lawyer proceeds on the premise that the facts are as the client tells them to him." Does this mean that Advocates are less likely to examine the client's story carefully? Apparently so. For while 31 per cent of the Advocates said that it was *not* the job of a lawyer to investigate his marital client's story, only 13 per cent of the Counselors took this stand. And, conversely, while 34 per cent of the Counselors indicated that investigating the client's story was part of a lawyer's role, only 15 per cent of the Advocates agreed. The evidence suggests, then, that Advocates and Counselors have distinctly different attitudes in this matter. Here are the pertinent remarks of two Advocates:

A lawyer doesn't know if the client's story is true and he doesn't care. He simply prepares the papers on the assumption that it is true.

We are not supposed to be detectives. . . . I can't disbelieve my client; it's not my job.

Counselors take quite a different view:

A lawyer must ascertain the truth for himself.

It's part of a lawyer's job to figure out what is really going on in any given situation.

Although these two attitudes represent conflicting points of view, each is compatible with one of the role definitions. The Counselor's definition requires an attorney to take an active part in defining and solving the client's problem; we would expect him to scrutinize the client's story more carefully than the Advocate, who, primarily concerned with fulfilling the client's desires, is apt to accept the story as given.

Role definitions aside, a lawyer's attitude toward the probable accuracy of his client's story is influenced by a number of other considerations. For example, he is not obliged, legally or ethically, to represent only clients whose stories he believes to be true.[9] Furthermore, he is not unaffected by the court's attitude. He is apt to believe—as was pointed out in Chapter 2—that judges grant decrees in matrimonial actions even though they may privately doubt the validity of the evidence presented. A lawyer may, therefore, reach the conclusion stated by one attorney: "If people meet the requirements of the statute, they are entitled to their divorce or annulment. Of course their stories look funny. . . . But you know the judges figure that these people are finished with each other; they want a divorce. So what difference does it make?" A lawyer may also find that it is extremely difficult to discover the truth about his client's marital conflict. Usually, he has only the testimony of the client and witnesses who, in most cases, are close friends and relatives of the client. And even should there be no deliberate falsification of facts, spouses may disagree honestly about the events in their marriage. Granted that all of these considerations condition an attorney's assessment of clients' stories, our evidence indicates that his attitude is determined principally by his role definition. To fulfill his role obligations, the Counselor is more likely to strive for accurate information about his client's problem than the Advocate.

An attorney's role definition also appears to affect his willingness to influence the decisions made by matrimonial clients. In discussing client-decisions our informants agreed on one general point: The client, not the lawyer, must make the decisions that affect that client; the lawyer's task is to indicate alternate paths of action. This position was summed up by one informant in this statement: "I tell clients what the facts are, what the law is, what the courts have done, and show them the alternatives. I tell them what the result of each alternative will be. Then I tell them they must decide." But what happens when the client cannot decide or seeks counsel's help? What is a lawyer's reaction to the situation described by one attorney? "After you lay out the facts and the alternatives, they immediately throw it back at you and say, 'You're the doctor.' " Our informants disagreed on how this problem should be dealt with. Two out of every three Advocates still insisted that they would not help the client to decide. Their attitude is expressed in these comments:

If the client is too upset to decide or can't be sure, I have a friend or relative, maybe a brother, come in and help her. I won't do it.

I don't help them to make decisions at all. They're the ones affected, not me. Besides, who is to say what a wrong decision is? What may be wrong for me or you, may be right for the client. I make them decide.

Counselors, on the other hand, are more inclined to aid the client; two out of every three said that they would attempt to induce the client to make what they thought was the right decision. "I try to persuade them," said one, "to do what is best for them."

Although they were disposed to participate in clients' decisions, Counselors varied somewhat in their willingness to do so. Some readily accepted decision-making as part of their role: "In these decisions your job is that of counselor. You point out that under these conditions this is an inordinate demand. You try and show that, while these decisions may seem right from the client's point of view, he'll only be back in court within months because it isn't fair and the other party will soon see it. You try and get the client to see the light." Other Counselors were more reluctant: "You try to get them to decide, but most of them want you to do it for them. So you finally decide in terms of what is best for the client, explaining carefully what is taking place."

When an attorney describes what he tries to do with a legal problem, he is, if only by implication, stating how he expects a client to behave. And when he describes client-behavior as interfering with his job, he is basing his description on his own role conception. Another consequence of our lawyers' role definitions is found in their complaints about marital clients. The complaint most frequently cited by Counselors—it was mentioned by one out of three—was the reluctance of marital clients to compromise. This kind of behavior, generated by client-emotionalism, conflicts with the Counselor's view of his role; the client is angry and vindictive while the lawyer is looking for a fair solution to the problem. One attorney remarked:

> There is a lack of compromise where an admirable settlement or arrangement may have been worked out by the lawyers. We may have worked out a neat solution to the visitation question but the client may insist that she doesn't want him to see the kids at all. Or there may be an adequate support arrangement for the children and the husband will back away because he is afraid the wife will get some of it. To the woman, "he's a bum," while the man is willing to do anything, "provided she doesn't get a cent." They want to win so badly, to drive such a hard bargain, that it is very hard to negotiate.

The unwillingness of marital clients to compromise was not considered by many Advocates to be much of an obstacle to their role performance; less than one out of ten referred to it. Their major complaint was directed to clients' indecisiveness. One out of three Advocates felt that client-uncertainty made it very difficult for a lawyer to do his job; only one out of ten Counselors made this complaint. An uncertain marital client is particularly troublesome to an Advocate because, as we reported, his role definition assumes that the client is certain. In the eyes of an Advocate, "a client must make up his mind before a lawyer can help him."

Correlates of Role Definitions

If we know that our informants differ in their role definitions, we now need to inquire into the sources of the difference. In this section, we examine the relationship between role definitions and other characteristics of our informants.

The concept of role orientation was introduced because we expected that it might affect a lawyer's conception of his task in a matrimonial action. The distribution of the informants' role definitions by their role orientations is shown in Table 4. There we see that people-oriented lawyers, technicians, and, to a lesser degree, trial lawyers are inclined to be Counselors; business organizers and money-oriented attorneys tend to be Advocates. In general, however, the effect of role orientation on role definition appears to be slight.

When role definitions are classified by attributes of legal practices, a discernible and consistent pattern emerges (see Table 5). Lawyers with specialized practices, for instance, are more likely than general practitioners to be Counselors. And, among the specialists, those with business practices are more apt to be Counselors than those with personal service practices. Further characteristics associated with being a Counselor are: a father who was a business executive or a professional; graduation from a university law school; and having a middle- or upper-class clientele. Being an Advocate, on the other hand, is associated with the following characteristics: a father who was a skilled or unskilled worker; graduation from a Catholic or independent law school; and having a working-class clientele.

Table 4: Distribution of Lawyers by Role Orientations and Role Definitions

ROLE ORIENTATION	*ROLE DEFINITION*		
	Counselor	*Advocate*	*Totals*[a]
Problem-oriented			
Trial lawyers	11	6	17
Technicians	13	2	15
Organizers	1	2	3
People-oriented	15	4	19
Money-oriented	4	7	11
Totals	44	21	65

[a] Excludes nine lawyers who reported role definitions other than Counselor and Advocate and eight lawyers who could not be classified by role orientation.

Looking at the comparison of role definitions and types of matrimonial practice, we see that lawyers with peripheral practices were more likely to be Counselors than those with major practices, who, in turn, were more apt to be Counselors than lawyers with minor matrimonial practices.

To account for this general pattern, we need to recall a point made in our earlier discussion of legal practice. We stated that law practices could be characterized as producing different degrees of security in professional work; practices vary insofar as lawyers can be sure of future cases. General practice, we said, seems to be comparatively insecure; and a general practitioner usually

Table 5: Role Definitions by Attributes of Law Practice, in Per Cent [a]

ATTRIBUTES OF LAW PRACTICE	ROLE DEFINITION		
	Counselor	Advocate	Number in Group [b]
Organization of practice			
Solo	63	37	(41)
Partnership	69	31	(32)
Type of law school attended			
University	71	29	(24)
Catholic	58	42	(19)
Independent	63	37	(30)
Lawyers' fathers' occupation			
Professional and business executive	79	21	(19)
Small business and "white collar"	60	40	(40)
Skilled and unskilled labor	57	43	(14)
Clients' class background			
Upper	75	25	(16)
Middle	73	27	(22)
Working	54	46	(35)
Types of cases [c]			
General	56	44	(25)
Personal service	62	38	(16)
Business	74	26	(23)
Types of matrimonial practice			
Peripheral	81	19	(16)
Minor	59	41	(41)
Major	63	37	(16)

[a] Per cents are added horizontally.
[b] Excludes nine lawyers who reported role definitions other than Counselor and Advocate.
[c] Excludes nine lawyers with specialties in both personal service and business cases.

must accept any case he receives. In fully or semi-specialized practice, the insecurity is less; a lawyer, by concentrating in a particular field of law, becomes known to other lawyers whose referrals, combined with those from past clients, make his future work less problematic. Finally, we noted that if specialization involves a clientele with continual need of legal service, an attorney's work takes on a relatively high degree of security. We suggest that it is this variation in professional security that largely determines an attorney's role definition in matrimonial cases. Lawyers with relatively insecure practices are apt to adhere to the well-structured role of the Advocate, while those with more secure practices will tend to adhere to the less-structured, and from counsel's point of view, more independent role of the Counselor.

If this interpretation is correct, a lawyer's relationship to his matrimonial client would appear to be a special instance of a broader empirical generalization: uncertain working conditions tend to elicit among workers a marked preference for well-defined roles.[10]

The Problem of Reconciliation

Several different points of view have been expressed by members of the legal profession about the problem of reconciliation in matrimonial cases. The authors of Survey of the Legal Profession assume that an attorney should strive to reconcile clients with their spouses.[11] Indeed, they assert that "it is common knowledge among leaders of the bar that the average lawyer will try his best to reunite estranged couples and to prevent divorce before agreeing to institute legal proceedings." [12] Others have argued that it is unrealistic to expect lawyers, especially if they handle many matrimonial cases, to attempt reconciliation because it is not remunerative work.[13] Still others have implied that attorneys possess neither the training nor the skill to recognize whether or not spouses can or should be reconciled.[14] In addition, it has been argued that the adversary nature of legal proceedings virtually precludes reconciliation in all but a few cases.[15] Considering the divergence of opinion on this subject, it is important to bear in mind that a lawyer is not required, either by law or by the canons of professional ethics, to advise for or against reconciliation.[16]

We discussed the problem of reconciliation with our informants. Though most of them did not include it in their role definitions, a majority—three out of five—said that a lawyer should explore the possibility of reconciliation before proceeding with a matrimonial action. However, while Counselors were more disposed than Advocates to take this position, both were equally pessimistic about a lawyer's chances for success. Almost two-thirds (64 per cent) of the Counselors believed that a lawyer should attempt reconciliation; less than half (46 per cent) of the Advocates held this belief. Yet 59 per cent of the Counselors and 56 per cent of the Advocates also believed that a lawyer's reconciliatory efforts would *not* generally be successful. In fact, only 8 per cent of the Counselors and 4 per cent of the Advocates thought that counsel could help reunite couples in most matrimonial cases.*

These findings suggest that for most of our informants, the problem of reconciliation involves a question of professional norm priority. The norms that define the

* Thirty-three per cent of the counselors and 42 per cent of the advocates were undecided as to whether or not attorneys could generally reconcile matrimonial clients with their spouses.

Counselor and Advocate roles are, in general, given higher priority than the norm of reconciliation. This differential in norm priority grows out of the cross-pressures of law practice, pressures that both motivate and inhibit attempts at reconciliation. Six such pressures were identified in reviewing the interview protocols.

1. THE ACCEPTANCE OF THE NORM It is probably true that when people accept a normative expectation as legitimate they will attempt to conform to it. When most of our informants identify themselves as lawyers, they believe they have an obligation to examine reconciliation as a possible solution in matrimonial cases.

I always try and see if reconciliation is possible before going ahead. I believe it is an important part of my job. I feel that *it is part of a lawyer's job.*

A lawyer should try. I always try. . . . Sometimes it works . . . not generally.

A lawyer is not likely to succeed in most cases. But *he should try* and *I think most of us do.* Certainly, he ought not to let the idea of a fee deter him.

As these excerpts make plain, the norm is perceived as applying to the professional's status. It is more than a personal inclination; not just "my job," but "part of a lawyer's job." And it is believed that the norm is conformed to throughout the profession: "Most of us do." Furthermore, the norm is complied with despite the recognition of obstacles—"A lawyer is not likely to succeed"—and countervailing pressures—"He ought not to let the idea of a fee deter him."

2. LAWYERS' PERSONAL SENTIMENTS As husbands and fathers, as sons and brothers, attorneys share with clients many significant cultural norms about marriage and family life. Hence, they often react to matrimonial

clients not only as professionals but as individuals with similar social ties and with potentially similar problems. Given their own familial commitments, they are not insensitive to the consequences of matrimonial actions. "As a human being," said one informant, "you hate to see a marriage break up." Because they share important values with matrimonial clients, lawyers can derive a deep gratification from their participation in reconciliation.[17] This may prompt attorneys to make strong efforts to reunite estranged spouses. Here is one lawyer's description of what he called "the most satisfying thing that ever happened to me in practice":

A couple had been married for thirty years and were going to break up. . . . I kept after both of them, and it finally worked out. . . . I'd run into them on the street, walking to a movie arm in arm and I'd have a real glow, a tremendous sense of satisfaction. I didn't get a penny for it. He wanted to pay something, but how can you put a price on a thing like that?

3. THE PRAGMATICS OF PRACTICE Even should a lawyer reject the norm of reconciliation on the ground that it is not part of his role, or that it represents at best a futile gesture, he may be forced into examining the problem simply to protect his own interests. When there is any likelihood that his client may be reconciled with the spouse, he may be reluctant to devote his time to the case. He may therefore comply with the norm in order to be sure that the marriage will be dissolved:

We search the matter of reconciliation out as a possibility but really don't expect anything to come of it. It's much too late by then. *But the important thing is that I don't want to go ahead and work on a matter if it isn't going through. I don't want to work for nothing.*

The first thing I do is to look into the possibility that a reconcilation may occur. I do this not because I'm a marriage counselor. *I just don't want to waste my time if they are not certain.*

The attitude expressed here need not mean that a lawyer will engage in merely perfunctory efforts at reconciliation. His concern with his own schedule of work elicits a genuine interest in knowing what the client plans to do.[18]

4. THE EXPERIENCE OF FAILURE Very few informants believed that a lawyer actually could successfuly reconcile estranged spouses. "My job should be to try and reconcile them," remarked one lawyer, "and I always see if it is possible, but there's no chance as a rule." His judgment was shared by most of the informants whose experience with reconciliation attempts was largely one of failure:

I must report to you sadly that in thirty-two years, no matter how hard I tried, there were very few, only a very few reconciliations.

It's a little too late by the time I see them. In ten years I've had two reconciliations, but they didn't last.

The experience of failure would seem to be a strong pressure undermining the norm of reconciliation; and the reason why lawyers define their roles without including the norm is clear: men are not likely to give high saliency to a norm so far out of line with experience.

5. THE CLIENT: SYMBOL OF A DEAD MARRIAGE Another pressure subverting the norm of reconciliation is the belief that identifies the presence of the marital client with the termination of his marriage. Slightly more than one out of five informants spontaneously asserted

that if an individual sees a lawyer about his marital conflict, it is only a matter of time before the marriage is dissolved: "People don't come to a lawyer to be reconciled. Generally reconciliation is out or they don't see a lawyer." This belief, mentioned equally by Counselors and Advocates, is based on the assumption that people first go through some kind of formal or informal institutional machinery in order to renew their marriages, and that only then, do they come to an attorney:

> The spouses probably tried reconciliation themselves. After all, no one wants to admit failure in such a situation. It isn't easy to break up a marriage relationship. Then you'll find that the family and friends of the couple have tried because they hate to see the break-up.
>
> By the time these people get to a lawyer, they have seen psychiatrists, they've talked to friends, counselors, rabbis, priests. Once they decide to see a lawyer, it's over.

The mechanisms employed by various segments of the public to obtain help with marital problems is a topic about which little is known. However, by assuming that such mechanisms are used, lawyers would seem to relieve themselves of some of the responsibility for effecting reconciliations: they become, in effect, professionals, who, through a division of labor, are responsible for burying legally what others have diagnosed as socially dead. There is also the possibility that, in an unknown proportion of cases, lawyers, by believing that their clients' marriages are beyond rehabilitation, may be contributing to the dissolution of those marriages. This is the familiar process of a "self-fulfilling prophecy": "A false definition of the situation" evokes "behavior which makes the originally false conception come true." [19] If the active intervention of a court can save some marriages after spouses have hired their attorneys,[20] then the belief that a marital client symbolizes an irreconcilable marriage warrants careful study.

6. THE LACK OF COMPETENCY An attorney's attitude toward reconciliation is apt to be influenced by his sense of competency. There was no doubt in the minds of some informants that lawyers lack the necessary professional preparation: "No lawyer is trained or equipped to decide who should live together and who should not." This conviction was supported by lawyers' recognition that reconciliation is not a simple task, and that other professionals are trained to cope with it:

> We are not equipped to do it. We're not sociologists [sic] or marriage counselors. Reconciliation is a complicated business and lawyers are just not equipped to do it.

But this is more than a matter of inadequate training; as we pointed out earlier, the legal training that a lawyer receives and its application in the lawyer-client relationship tend to minimize the chances of reconciliation occurring. Not only does an attorney lack the skills of a psychiatrist or social worker, in his trained capacity as a lawyer he is expected to represent one side of a conflict. Thus, even when opposing counsel try to reconcile their clients, they do so without adequate professional preparation and within a context where each is held responsible only for his own client's interest.

SUMMARY AND IMPLICATIONS FOR FURTHER RESEARCH

CHAPTER 7

In this monograph we have studied some of the pressures impinging on private professional practitioners by examining matrimonial law practice among a group of New York lawyers. We conclude now with a brief summary of our findings and some suggestions for further research.

In Chapter 2 we discussed the cultural context of matrimonial practice. We noted that a conflict exists between legal theory and public attitudes concerning matrimonial dissolutions. During the past hundred years, the rate of marital disruption has greatly increased, and while the public has become more tolerant of divorce and remarriage, the legal norms governing the termination of marriage have not changed. As a result, there has emerged a widespread institutionalized evasion of these legal norms. This evasion creates a professional role conflict for lawyers who are simultaneously expected to uphold the law and represent clients intent on ending their marriages. The role conflict is alleviated somewhat by two attitudes prevailing among lawyers: (1) It is the general professional consensus that matrimonial laws are ineffectual; and (2) many members of the bench and bar tacitly recognize that the evasion of matrimonial laws achieves a socially desired end.

We noted that this cultural conflict is particularly acute in New York State because of two conditions. First, the state's rate of marital disruption is higher than the national average. Second, New York has a conservative divorce law and a liberal annulment law. These factors are responsible for three patterns of evasion engaged in by many New Yorkers: some establish temporary residences in other states to secure divorces; others initiate annulment rather than divorce actions in New York; still others obtain New York divorces through collusion, subornation, and perjury.

Finally, evidence was presented showing that practicing New York attorneys were extremely critical of their state's matrimonial laws, that they recognized and privately accepted evasion of those laws, and that they found their participation in matrimonial cases a disturbing and frustrating experience.

Since cultural pressures do not directly influence behavior but are mediated by structural variables, we turned, in Chapter 3, to a discussion of the social context of legal practice. We began by observing that the urban demand for specialized legal services, the growth and complexity of legal knowledge, financial incentives, and competitive pressures were molding a type of law work far removed from the traditional image of practice. The solo general practitioner, who knew and was known to most people in a small town, is now more of an exception than ever. Increasingly, the modern lawyer is a specialist working with other lawyers in large urban centers.

We also indicated that a highly imperfect formal competition is characteristic of contemporary law practice. A lawyer's ability to compete with members of the profession depends, to a considerable degree, on status attributes that have nothing technically to do with legal ability. Evidence was adduced to show that ethnic, religious, and sex attributes partly determine the type of law school attended, the kind of initial employment obtained, and the type of practice established.

Following this overview of modern law practice, we reported the types of practices engaged in by lawyers in our sample. Three types were identified: general, concentrated, and specialized. Each of these types differed from the others in designated ways. Briefly summarized, the differences were as follows: (1) General practitioners were more likely to practice alone than lawyers with partly or fully specialized practices; (2) although there were important exceptions, attorneys with concentrated or completely specialized practices were in practice much longer than general practitioners; (3) lawyers in general practice were more apt to come from lower social strata than other lawyers; (4) while general practitioners depended heavily on working-class clients, those with concentrated or specialized practices drew their clients mostly from the middle and upper classes; (5) although general practices were the most diversified, they were built primarily around matrimonial, commercial, real estate, negligence, and criminal cases; (6) practices with some degree of specialization were centered around either personal service cases (matrimonial, negligence, and criminal) or business cases (commercial, corporation, and real estate).

These characteristics of legal practice are important, we noted, because they are associated with varying degrees of professional security. To clarify this association, we introduced a distinction between permanent and transitory clients and suggested that it might be useful to view a law practice as a community of clients. In some instances, the community is relatively stable; it includes an essentially permanent clientele so that counsel can be reasonably sure of future legal work. In other instances, where the clientele is mostly transitory, the community is comparatively unstable, and counsel can never be certain of the number or nature of future cases. Our analysis of the interview data led us to conclude that practices concentrated or specialized in business cases were the most secure, that specialized personal service practices were less secure, and that general practices were the least secure.

The significance of security in practice was illustrated by our discussion of cases that were accepted by lawyers even when they preferred to reject them. Acceptance of disliked cases was most prevalent among the general practitioners. The reasons given by the informants for taking such cases were more instructive. General practitioners accepted the cases because they needed the fees; specialists accepted them to render a personal favor to regular clients, relatives, or friends.

In Chapter 4, we shifted our attention to patterns of matrimonial practice. Three types of matrimonial practice were reported by the informants. For some lawyers matrimonial cases were largely peripheral to their law practices. These attorneys not only handled relatively few such cases—usually less than four a year—they did not regard the cases as part of their normal work. The few matrimonial actions with which they did deal were accepted as a personal service to regular clients, relatives, or friends.

Most informants had minor matrimonial practices in which the cases played neither a central nor a peripheral part in their practice of law. Although there was some yearly variation, these lawyers generally participated in about a dozen matrimonial cases annually; correlatively, they perceived the cases as constituting a small but definite part of their professional work. These minor practices were sustained primarily through the referrals of past matrimonial clients, and the cases were accepted because they represented a small but necessary source of income.

Still other informants had major matrimonial practices. These major practitioners reported that they handled anywhere from twenty-five to fifty matrimonial cases each year. Nearly all of them identified themselves as matrimonial specialists. While they relied partly on the recommendations of past clients, their main referral sources were other members of the bar. Matrimonial cases were accepted by these specialists not only because they constituted a chief source of income, but because the cases were identified with law practice.

We then considered the relationship between types of legal practice and types of matrimonial practice. More concretely, we noted that most of the general practitioners had minor matrimonial practices, most lawyers who concentrated or specialized in business cases had peripheral practices, and most of those whose work was centered around personal service cases had major matrimonial practices. In addition, we reported that no informant had initially planned to engage in his specific type of matrimonial practice; the various patterns of matrimonial work were largely the result of the exigencies of law practice.

Our analysis of the relationship between types of legal practice and types of matrimonial practice revealed two significant findings. In the first place, matrimonial cases have different consequences for different types of practitioners. Otherwise put, the same kind of legal case serves different functions in different kinds of law practices. In general practice, the primary function of a matrimonial case is the partial contribution it makes to counsel's income. The relative diversity of his work means that a general practitioner is financially dependent on several kinds of cases, no one of which he can afford to ignore. In business practices, on the other hand, these cases serve a quite different function. Concerned principally with problems of commercial and corporate law, business practitioners neither need nor personally desire matrimonial cases. However, to maintain the good will of their regular business clients, they accept the matrimonial cases recommended by these clients. In this context, the handling of the cases serves the function of maintaining the relationship between attorneys and their nonmatrimonial clienteles. In major matrimonial practices, the cases serve still other functions. Beyond supplying counsel with a principal source of income, they provide the basis for claiming the professional image of specialist.

The second significant finding relates to our earlier discussion of the cultural context of matrimonial practice, a context, it will be recalled, that involved a conflict between legal theory and public attitudes. We pointed out that the context in New York was avoided by clients who could afford to leave the state and obtain a migratory divorce elsewhere. But a client's ability to leave the state also affects his lawyer. Consequently, we found that not all informants participated equally in New York matrimonial actions. As we also pointed out, this differential participation was due to a variation in the class background of legal clienteles. Accordingly, general practitioners, with their large proportion of working-class clients, were more apt to handle New York actions than other lawyers. Attorneys with business and personal service practices, representing primarily middle- and upper-class clients, were more likely than general practitioners to send their marital clients out of state. In short, because they engage in different types of law practices, lawyers are influenced differently by the cultural context of matrimonial practice.

In Chapter 5 we reported and discussed at length how attorneys perceived and evaluated matrimonial cases. Their professional imagery of the cases fall into three main categories: characteristics of clients, dimensions of matrimonial problems, and the effects of the cases on lawyers. The most salient image of matrimonial clients reported by our informants referred to client-emotionalism: the feelings, attitudes, and overt behavior of distraught husbands and wives. Although they recognized the sources of this emotionalism, attorneys found that it often evoked in clients demands for excessively partisan representation, vengeful behavior, and attempts to involve counsel personally in the case. Furthermore, we noted that two kinds of professional role behavior frequently intensified client-emotionalism. First, efforts by counsel to obtain relevant facts from clients often allowed the latter to see in greater detail how unhappy their marriages were. Second, in attempting to demonstrate to the courts that their clients will probably succeed in the anticipated action, lawyers feel compelled to prepare affidavits in which clients are encouraged to spell out their grievances against their spouses in vivid and unmistakable terms.

Other types of clients, we observed, also manifest some degree of emotionalism, but the interpersonal context of matrimonial actions apparently generates more emotional behavior than most lawyers are accustomed to. Indeed, some informants felt that matrimonial clients were mentally ill. At any rate, our analysis of the image of client-emotionalism led us to conclude that attorneys are not professionally equipped to cope with matrimonial clients, and that, as far as this type of legal problem is concerned, they suffer from "trained incapacity."

According to our informants, matrimonial clients are not only emotional, they are ignorant: ignorant of the law, ignorant of a lawyer's role, and ignorant of their own intentions. This ignorance, which was the second reported client-image, compounds the difficulty lawyers experience in dealing with matrimonial clients. Clients may be ignorant in other types of cases, we noted, but at least in other cases attorneys have some guide, a rough blueprint, that permits them to judge what clients will probably do and what their clients' best interests are. In matrimonial cases, however, there are no equivalent guides. As a result, attorneys report that it is difficult to explain to these clients the requirements of the law, what the role of counsel involves, and the legal rights of the opposing side.

The third client-image cited by lawyers referred to the difficulty they encountered in representing female clients. They attributed this image to the fact that marital disruption has a greater emotional impact on wives than husbands, and that the former generally have less legal experience than the latter. In addition, we pointed out that lawyers who represent wives in matrimonial actions are usually in the anomalous position of receiving their fees from opposing husbands. Although this does not normally alter the size of wife's counsel's fee, it often becomes a significant bargaining issue for attorneys on both sides.

A second set of images held by professionals of these cases was related to the nature of a matrimonial client's problem. Matrimonial cases were defined by a considerable number of informants as (1) personal and (2) nonlegal problems. As we reported, the image of a personal problem derives from three conditions present in these cases: The problem concerns clients in their private rather than public statuses; the problem has deep emotional significance for clients; and the solution to the problem inevitably affects significant primary group affiliations. While other kinds of cases involve important personal dimensions, they also include countervailing impersonal elements not usually found in matrimonial actions. Thus, the personal dimensions of tort and criminal cases may be diminished, though never eliminated, by the participation of insurance companies in the former and government officials and agencies in the latter.

The extremely personal nature of matrimonial cases was also related to the image of a nonlegal problem. In dealing with the personal issues of marital disruptions, our informants reportedly found little occasion to use their legal knowledge. What was required, they noted, was skill in handling interpersonal conflict.

The third set of professional images dealt with the effects of matrimonial cases on the participating lawyers. One image referred to the tendency of counsel to become personally involved in their clients' cases. The problem of involvement, our informants agreed, was encountered principally by lawyers who were not specialists in the cases. In discussing this image we considered how involvement was influenced by such factors as pressure from clients, alleged violations of important cultural norms, working on the details of clients' problems, the client's sex, the client's nonprofessional relationship to the lawyer, and the attorney's own familial relationships.

Another effect of these cases on lawyers was found in their image of strain, the sense of stress induced by trying to cope with emotional spouses. This stress was produced primarily by the excessive amount of time required to deal with these clients. This extra time, informants noted, tends to interfere with other legal work, involves expressions of personal reassurance rather than legal advice, and represents a service for which there is no adequate compensation. Moreover, informants who knew lawyers who rejected matrimonial cases said that the cases were avoided because of this strain.

Aside from client-emotionalism, the professional images of matrimonial cases varied by types of matrimonial practice. The images of the difficult female client and the personal problem were cited more frequently by peripheral practitioners than by others. For these lawyers, a female matrimonial client represented a sharp departure from their normal routine of dealing with male businessmen. Minor practitioners were more likely than other attorneys to mention the image of client-ignorance. We pointed out that minor practitioners were more dependent than other lawyers on working-class clients, clients with less education and legal experience than those from higher social strata. Finally, the image of strain was cited more frequently by major practitioners than by those with other types of matrimonial practice. The greater saliency of this image, we noted, did not necessarily mean that specialists experienced greater stress, but that their constant participation in these cases probably made them more aware than others of the image.

We concluded Chapter 5 by reporting the attitudes of our informants toward matrimonial cases. We noted that those who liked the cases explained their preference on the grounds that they enjoyed helping people with personal problems. Those who disliked the cases accounted for their attitude by citing the strain of handling them, the personal quality of the problems at stake, and the lack of adequate compensation. The attorneys who were indifferent stated that the cases were part of law practice, and, as such, were neither liked nor disliked. We also reported that these attitudes varied by type of matrimonial practice. In general, major practitioners liked them, peripheral practitioners disliked them, and minor practitioners were indifferent.

In Chapter 6 we considered how lawyers defined their roles in matrimonial actions. Since there was reason to believe that these role definitions would be affected by broader views of professional work, we began by discussing our informants' general role orientations toward law practice. Three major role orientations were identified. Some lawyers, we reported, were primarily oriented toward problems; they obtain most of their gratification in practice from the application of their skills to specific kinds of perplexing legal issues. Within this group, some attorneys were oriented chiefly toward trial work, others preferred research and analysis, and still others preferred organizing and reorganizing business enterprises. The second major role orientation involved an orientation toward people. Lawyers with this orientation sought primary gratification in their work from working with people. They were particularly interested in working on cases where clients were individuals rather than organizations, and where clients needed the help that they, as lawyers, could provide. Finally, some lawyers were mainly oriented toward money, and the gratification they received from practice was related not to problems or people but to the size of their fees.

When these role orientations were classified by other characteristics of our informants, the following patterns emerged: (a) Problem-oriented lawyers were more likely than others to have relatively high class origins, to have attended a university law school, to practice in partnerships, to have fairly affluent clients, and to engage in peripheral matrimonial practices; (b) people-oriented lawyers were more apt than other attorneys to have middle- and working-class backgrounds, to have attended Catholic and independent law schools, and to have personal service practices, often concentrating in matrimonial cases; (c) attorneys oriented toward money were more likely than others to have come from a working-class background, to have attended an independent law school, to be solo general practitioners, and to have minor matrimonial practices. These role orientations were also related to attitudes toward matrimonial cases. People-oriented lawyers were more inclined than others to like the cases, while problem-oriented attorneys either disliked or, like most of those with a money-orientation, were indifferent to the cases.

After discussing general role orientations, we turned to the question of role definitions in matrimonial actions. What do lawyers attempt to do for matrimonial clients? Our interview data revealed two distinct role definitions. The Counselor's definition is one in which the lawyer strives to control the relationship with his client by defining, to his own satisfaction, the substance of the client's problem, by arriving at his own judgment as to what constitute the client's best interests, and by guiding the client to a solution that is equitable for both spouses. In contrast, the Advocate's role is one in which counsel accepts the client's definition of the problem as well as the client's proposed solution. Furthermore, lawyers who adhere to the Advocate's role tend to see successful professional role performance as a victory over the opposing spouse. While most of the informants defined their role in matrimonial actions as that of Counselor, a substantial minority, almost one out of three, defined their role as Advocate.

We made two important points concerning these role definitions. First, they are not mutually exclusive; rather, each gives emphasis to different aspects of professional role behavior. Second, the Advocate's role, with its greater dependency on clients' wishes, seems to be more structured than the Counselor's role, where the exercise of professional judgment appears to introduce greater flexibility.

It was further suggested that these role definitions influence the interaction between lawyer and client. Evidence was presented to show (1) that Advocates tend to accept matrimonial clients' stories at face value, while Counselors make some effort to verify the stories; (2) that Advocates try to avoid helping clients make decisions, while Counselors attempt to influence their clients' decisions; and (3) that Advocates are more disturbed than Counselors when clients change their minds, while Counselors are more disturbed than Advocates when clients are reluctant to compromise.

To account for the differences in role definitions among the informants, we first classified them by role orientations. With one exception, role orientations appeared to make little difference. Both orientations toward problems and people, for instance, were highly associated with the Counselor's role. Only among money-oriented lawyers was there a preference for the Advocate's role. We then compared role definitions by other attributes of the informants. Our findings showed that most attorneys, no matter how they were classified, tended to adhere to the role of Counselor. However, within this over-all pattern there were important variations. Advocates were more apt than Counselors to come from a working-class background, to have attended a Catholic or independent law school, to be general practitioners, to have working-class clients, and to be engaged in minor matrimonial practices. Counselors, on the other hand, were more apt to come from the upper middle class, to have attended a university law school, to have business practices with upper-class clients, and to engage in peripheral matrimonial practices. In brief, the pressures that support the two role definitions seemed to vary with clusters of attributes associated with different types of law practices. We suggested that the combination of these attributes produced varying degrees of security in practice, and that it was the degree of security that directly determined a lawyer's role definition. Attorneys with relatively insecure practices preferred the comparatively well-structured role of the Advocate, while those with more secure practices preferred the less structured but professionally more independent role of Counselor. Among the informants, the Counselor's role was most frequently accepted by lawyers with peripheral matrimonial practices, less frequently by those with major practices, and least of all by minor practitioners. We then pointed out that an attorney's relationship with a matrimonial client appeared to be a special case of a broader empirical generalization: uncertain working conditions tend to evoke a preference for well-defined roles.

We concluded Chapter 6 with a discussion of the problem of reconciliation. Although most informants felt that a lawyer should explore the possibility of reconciliation whenever he handles a matrimonial case, most of them also reported that he is not likely to be successful. Our analysis showed that there were pressures in practice that both supported and subverted the norm of reconciliation, but that the latter pressures outweighed the former. The norm is supported, as we noted, by lawyers' acceptance of it and by their attempts to conform to it. It is also supported by lawyers' personal sentiments; most of them would be gratified if they could effect more reconciliations. Practical considerations further sustain the norm; attorneys need to be reasonably sure that the possibilities of reconciliation are remote in order to proceed with a client's legal action. On the other hand, the significance of the norm is undermined by attorneys' repeated failure to bring spouses together, by their belief that the process of consulting a lawyer symbolizes the end of the marriage, and by their recognition that reconciliatory efforts require professional skills that they do not possess.

The ideas and findings presented in this study have implications beyond the practice of law. They suggest at least four lines of inquiry which should add to our knowledge of the legal profession in contemporary life.

First of all, further research on the relationships between legal norms, public opinion, and the behavior of lawyers should contribute greatly to an understanding of the legal system, the practice of law, and the ways in which important social problems are handled. We described how the conflict between conservative law and liberal public attitudes is related to the evasion of law in matrimonial cases which produces a role dilemma for lawyers. What other types of cases generate this type of conflict? What mechanisms other than institutionalized evasion emerge to permit attorneys to cope with these kinds of situations? Furthermore, what are the consequences of these role conflicts and mitigating mechanisms for the legal system as a form of control? These queries might profitably be answered by examining cases where there is reason to believe that significant discrepancies exist in specific legal norms and attitudes characteristic of certain segments of society. Empirical studies of how lawyers handle cases involving insanity, obscenity, libel, and slander might be helpful in this respect. Perhaps even more instructive would be an examination of the administration of laws prohibiting religious and racial discrimination. This latter inquiry would have the added merit of illustrating a cultural context in which liberal laws are often at odds with public opinion.

A second line of inquiry is suggested by our finding that matrimonial cases serve diverse functions in different types of legal practice. This finding, which undoubtedly holds true for other types of cases, draws attention to the obvious fact that attorneys are not exposed equally to various kinds of legal problems. What are the consequences of this fact for the profession as a whole? In particular, what are its effects on the activities of bar associations? Here we would need to know what kinds of lawyers participate actively in their professional organizations. We would expect to find patterned variation in participation. This might mean that some types of practitioners—possibly those in corporate and commercial practice—are overrepresented in bar activities, while others—perhaps general practitioners and those specializing in personal service cases—are underrepresented. If this turned out to be true, it then would be extremely important to explore the relationships between bar association policies on such matters as legal reform, professional ethics, and legal education, and to examine the professional experiences of those who speak in the name of the bar. It may well be that the views expressed by the organized bar reflect in a reasonably accurate way the experiences of certain types of practitioners, while ignoring or even distorting the experiences of other types of lawyers. Should this prove to be the case, it would raise additional questions concerning the bar's ability to control professional behavior, its capacity to judge the effectiveness of legal norms, and its sensitivity to the legal needs of all segments of the public.

A third kind of study is indicated by our finding that, in handling matrimonial cases, lawyers appear to suffer from a trained incapacity. The issue at stake is not simply whether lawyers can or should be taught explicitly to deal with highly emotional clients; rather, it has to do with the broader question of how attorneys acquire the skills and knowledge for coping with any legal problem. The question involves two lines of research. First, how is knowledge acquired and applied in specific kinds of cases? To what extent is a lawyer's professional "know-how" influenced by his law school training, his friends and acquaintances in practice, his use of how-to-do-it manuals, his role orientation, and his personality characteristics? Secondly, how are the prevailing conceptions of legal knowledge affected by knowledge in nonlegal fields? If it is clear that the behavior of scientists, doctors, clergymen, and other men of knowledge is partly controlled by law, it is also true that members of the legal profession are guided in their professional activities by nonlegal knowledge. But what kinds of nonlegal concepts and data are willingly accepted, perhaps defined as common sense, what kinds are used reluctantly, and what kinds are rejected? Correlatively, what pressures motivate what types of practitioners to examine some and not other fields of intellectual work outside of law? In general, we need to find out how lawyers perceive their clients' needs, and how this perception is related to lawyers' images and evaluations of other professions. When obtained, such data should enable us not only to understand how attorneys acquire the skills they use and those they neglect, but how the legal system controls and is controlled by the knowledge available in society.

Finally, further explorations of lawyers' professional role orientations should help us understand what law practice means to those who practice. Beyond those reported in this monograph, what are some of the other possible orientations toward law work? What are the psychological and social determinants and consequences of various orientations for lawyers, their clients, and the profession? To what extent are these orientations influenced by increased specialization and group practice?

Similar queries can be raised concerning role definitions. Moreover, we should begin to find out whether role definitions are more characteristic of lawyers or cases. For example, do some attorneys always attempt to play the Advocate or Counselor while others shift their role with certain types of cases? And how are these role definitions affected by clients' attributes? Do attorneys change their role definitions to cope with clients who vary by sex, age, race, religion, class position, and ethnic background?

These are but a few of the questions suggested by our study of matrimonial practice. They are enough, however, to warrant the belief that both lawyers and sociologists would benefit by further research on the practice of law. It will, we believe, become increasingly difficult for members of the bar to ignore the ideas and techniques of sociological inquiry, especially if such inquiry is designed to inform them of the behavior of lawyers and clients. And surely it is time that American sociologists begin systematically to look at, and to learn from, the men who apply the law to the problems of men.

SAMPLE CHARACTERISTICS

APPENDIX A

This appendix presents additional characteristics of our sample of eighty-two lawyers. It should be kept in mind that the sample was drawn to provide a group representative of New York attorneys who deal with matrimonial cases. It is not representative of all lawyers practicing law in New York City.

	(*per cent*)
1. *Sex*	
Male	95
Female	5
2. *Race*	
White	91
Negro	9
3. *Marital Status*	
Married	95
Single	5
4. *Religious Background*	
Jewish	80
Protestant	11
Catholic	9

5. *Age.* The lawyers' ages ranged from twenty-eight to seventy-eight years. The median age was forty-nine years.

6. *Years in Practice.* The number of years in practice ranged from four to fifty-six years. The median number of years in practice was twenty-three.

7. *Status in Practice*

	(*per cent*)
Solo	58
Partner	38
Associate	4

8. *Law School Background.* Of these lawyers, 33 per cent attended university law schools, 24 per cent went to Catholic law schools, and 43 per cent attended independent law schools. The names of these law schools and the number of attorneys who attended each follow.

University Law Schools	
Columbia	10
Cornell	1
Harvard	3
Howard	1
New York University	12
Catholic Law Schools	
Fordham	6
St. John's	14
Independent Law Schools	
Brooklyn	21
New York	14

9. *Sample Bias.* Seventeen lawyers in our original sample of ninety-nine were not interviewed. As we reported, one had died, six refused to be interviewed, and ten had schedules that made interviewing impractical. Since we lack information on all of these practitioners, we cannot tell if their absence seriously biased the results. We were able to find out from legal directories the professional education and the approximate length of time in practice for eight of these attorneys, whose inclusion in the study would not have altered in any sig-

nificant way the distribution of informants by type of law school and length of time in practice. This still, of course, leaves nine other attorneys unaccounted for. It is our hunch—and it is at best a hunch—that most of these nine were either salaried employees with part-time private practices or lawyers with essentially neighborhood clienteles. If there is a bias in our sample, it may be due to the underrepresentation of these two kinds of practitioners.

A NOTE ON THE INTERVIEWS

APPENDIX B

Anyone who gathers data through the use of interviews, questionnaires, or participant observation must first be accepted by those who are to give the necessary information. This is not to say that the technical nature of the research goals must be understood by those who are to be studied; but their willingness to cooperate usually depends on their ability to grasp, in a broad sense, what the researcher is trying to do. In this study of matrimonial practice there were grounds for wondering whether or not lawyers would cooperate.

First, it was conceivable that questions pertaining to the actual practice of law could be defined as an invasion of professional confidence. If, for example, an attorney were asked to illustrate a particular kind of problem that emerged in his dealings with clients, the question could be misinterpreted as an effort to seek information on specific clients. Second, it was possible that lawyers would be reluctant to discuss their work with anyone not trained in law. At best, such reluctance might be based on the conviction that a layman could not possibly understand their professional problems; at worst, lawyers could ascribe a variety of base motives to a non-legal researcher. Third, the fact that we wished to examine in particular matrimonial practice, with all its well known discrepancies between legal theory and actual behavior, could easily have silenced attorneys who might be willing to talk of other aspects of practice.

Since all but a few attorneys in the sample participated willingly, it may be instructive to review briefly our preliminary steps taken prior to each interview.

Each lawyer was initially reached by telephone, and briefly given the rationale for the research which was generally accepted as reasonable. Aside from stating the purpose of the study, this explanation included a statement of how the lawyer's name had been obtained and the identification of the researcher as a sociologist affiliated with a major university. As we noted, some refused to participate. One replied: "You must think I'm crazy." Another wanted to know, "What kind of gag is this?" These were the exceptions; most agreed immediately to be interviewed.

At the beginning of every interview, the researcher presented his credentials: a letter of introduction from the chairman of the Sociology Department of Columbia University and another letter from the Social Science Research Council. The general purpose of the research was stated once again. Each lawyer was then informed that his remarks would be treated with the strictest confidence, and that we were in no way interested in any particular clients or cases. The general impression that we attempted to communicate can be described in the following way: As sociologists, we are interested in group behavior. Lawyers constitute an important group in society. We are interested in some of the problems lawyers encounter in their work, particularly in the handling of matrimonial cases. You, as a member of the legal profession, can help us by answering a few questions. This was, of course, our own definition of the interviewing situation, and it explains why we refer to the interviewed lawyers as informants, rather than as respondents or interviewees. It is our impression that most of the informants defined the study as an investigation of one facet of the divorce problem and not primarily as a study of law practice. In any event, most of them seemed to take the position that sociologist and lawyer were sharing a problem of mutual concern.

The fact that most attorneys in the sample were cooperative does not mean that we should have taken such cooperation for granted. In a number of instances, lawyers we had interviewed said that initially they had had some doubts concerning our motives. Some wondered whether or not we were conducting an investigation for a bar association; others thought that we might be preparing a series of articles for a local newspaper. And one informant was almost certain that we were hired by a client's husband to ascertain his strategy in a pending divorce case. Whenever such doubts were reported, three questions were put to the lawyers: Were their answers given during the interview colored by their doubts? What persuaded them that their doubts were unrealistic? What could be done in future interviews to eliminate such doubts? In every case we were informed that their doubts did not influence their answers; that they were convinced upon finding the questions unrelated to their fears; and that they knew of no way of alleviating such doubts in the future. It is difficult to estimate what effect, if any, these doubts had on the interview situation. We can only point out that there were no obvious differences between the replies given by the lawyers who originally had doubts and the ones who had none. Since a few informants explicitly stated their initial misgivings, it is probably wise to assume that there were others with similar feelings but failed to mention them. This raises a more general question pertaining to the validity of the interview material.

How do we know that the attorneys in our sample gave us truthful answers? Is it not reasonable to believe that, when questioned about such a professionally sensitive subject as matrimonial practice, lawyers might understandably be less than candid? There are at least three reasons for believing that the data obtained in the interviews reflect accurately the informants' perceptions of their professional experiences, opinions, and attitudes. It is doubtful, first of all, that many lawyers would interrupt their work routines to spend an hour or so deliberately giving an interviewer misleading information. Second, there was substantial consensus among most informants on many of the topics discussed in the interview—different lawyers consistently gave similar answers to our queries. Finally, many of the answers and comments provided by these attorneys could have been anticipated, in a loose and unsystematic way, by anyone who had made a careful study of the available literature on matrimonial practice.

NOTES

Chapter 1

1. Logan Wilson, *The Academic Man* (New York: Oxford University Press, 1942); Paul F. Lazarsfeld and Wagner Thielens, Jr., *The Academic Mind* (Glencoe, Ill.: The Free Press, 1958); Alfred H. Stanton and Morris S. Schwartz, *The Mental Hospital* (New York: Basic Books, Inc., 1954); William Caudill, *The Psychiatric Hospital as a Small Society* (Cambridge, Mass.: Harvard University Press, 1958); Mary E. W. Gross, "Influence and Authority Among Physicians in an Outpatient Clinic," *American Sociological Review,* XXVI (February, 1961), 39–50; Joseph Ben-David, "The Professional Role of the Physician in Bureaucratized Medicine," *Human Relations,* XI (August, 1958), 255–74; Mark G. Field, *Doctor and Patient in Soviet Russia* (Cambridge, Mass.: Harvard University Press, 1957); Harold L. Wilensky, *Intellectuals in Labor Unions* (Glencoe, Ill.: The Free Press, 1956). See also Robert K. Merton, *Social Theory and Social Structure,* rev. ed. (Glencoe, Ill.: The Free Press, 1957), pp. 207–24; Donald C. Pelz, "Some Social Factors Related to Performance in a Research Organization," *Administrative Science Quarterly,* I (December, 1956), 310–25; and Leonard Reissman, "A Study of Role Conceptions in Bureaucracy," *Social Forces,* XXVI (March, 1949), 305–10.
2. See, for example, Roy Lewis and Angus Maude, *Professional People in England* (Cambridge, Mass.: Harvard University Press, 1953), pp. 261–70; Ben-David, *op. cit.,* pp. 259–60; C.

Wright Mills, *White Collar* (New York: Oxford University Press, 1951), Chap. VI, especially p. 114; A. M. Carr-Saunders and P. A. Wilson, *The Professions* (London: Oxford University Press, 1933), pp. 478, 501–503.

3. There is some empirical material bearing on private practice. See Oswald Hall's three articles: "The Informal Organization of the Medical Profession," *Canadian Journal of Economics and Sociology,* XII (1946), 30–44; "The Stages of a Medical Career," *American Journal of Sociology,* LIII (March, 1948), 327–36; "Types of Medical Careers," *American Journal of Sociology,* LV (November, 1949), 243–53; Stanley Lieberson, "Ethnic Groups and the Practice of Medicine," *American Sociological Review,* XXIII (October, 1958), 542–49; Eliot Freidson, "Client Control in Medical Practice," *American Journal of Sociology,* LXV (January, 1960), 374–82; William Henry Hale, *Career Development of the Negro Lawyer in Chicago* (unpublished Ph.D. dissertation, Department of Sociology, University of Chicago, 1949); Walter I. Wardell and Arthur L. Wood, "Informal Relations in the Practice of Criminal Law," *American Journal of Sociology,* LXII (July, 1956), 48–55; Dan C. Lortie, "Laymen to Lawmen: Law School Careers, and Professional Socialization," *Harvard Educational Review,* XXIX (Fall, 1959), 352–69. See also Jerome E. Carlin, *Lawyers on Their Own* (New Brunswick, N.J.: Rutgers University Press, 1962).
4. *The 1958 Distribution of Lawyers in the United States* (Chicago: American Bar Foundation, 1959).
5. Individual clients are, of course, commonly found in criminal and tort cases, but agents for private and public organizations usually participate in both types of actions. Today, a tort case that does not involve an insurance company is probably as rare as a criminal case without a prosecuting attorney.
6. Edward A. Ross, *Social Control* (New York: The Macmillan Co., 1928), p. 231; Talcott Parsons, rev. ed., *Essays in Sociological Theory* (Glencoe, Ill.: The Free Press, 1954), pp. 370–85.
7. Underhill Moore and Gilbert Sussman, "The Lawyer's Law," *Yale Law Review,* XLI (1931–32), 566. See also John R. Dos Passos, *The American Lawyer* (New York: Consolidated Law Book Co., Inc., 1919), pp. 70–71, and Charles A. Horsky, *The Washington Lawyer* (Boston: Little, Brown and Co., 1952), p. 126.
8. For some representative works see Paul H. Jacobson, *American Marriage and Divorce* (New York: Rinehart and Co., 1959);

Paul C. Glick, *American Families* (New York: John Wiley and Sons, Inc., 1957); William J. Goode, *After Divorce* (Glencoe, Ill.: The Free Press, 1956); Willard Waller, *The Family,* rev. ed. by Reuben Hill (New York: Dryden Press, 1951); Nathan Ackerman, *The Psychodynamics of Family Life* (New York: Basic Books, 1958).

9. For example, "A Symposium on Domestic Relations," *Vanderbilt Law Review,* IX (June, 1956); Maxine B. Virtue, *Family Cases in Court* (Durham, N.C.: Duke University Press, 1956); Morris Ploscowe, *The Truth About Divorce* (New York: Hawthorn Books, Inc., 1955); "Divorce—A Re-examination of Basic Concepts," *Law and Contemporary Problems,* XVIII (Winter, 1953); Walter Gellhorn, *Children and Families in the Courts of New York* (New York: Dodd, Mead and Co., 1954); *Conference on Divorce* (Chicago: University of Chicago Law School, 1952).
10. Marie W. Kargman, "The Lawyer as Divorce Counselor," *American Bar Association Journal,* XLVI (April, 1960), 399–401; Stanton L. Ehrlich, "What Is a Divorce Lawyer?" *Marriage and Family Living,* XXI (November, 1959), 361–66; Howard H. Spellman, *Successful Management of Matrimonial Cases* (New York: Prentice-Hall, Inc., 1954); Henry S. Drinker, "Problems of Professional Ethics in Matrimonial Litigation," *Harvard Law Review,* LXVI (January, 1953), 443–64; "The Lawyer as a Family Counselor," *The University of Kansas Law Review,* XXII (Fall, 1953), 28–53. For a rare attempt to study matrimonial practice empirically, see Joseph A. Gluckman, *The Role of the Lawyer in Matrimonial Cases* (unpublished Ph.D. dissertation, Teachers College, Columbia University, 1956). See also Carlin, *op. cit.,* pp. 91–101.
11. Leon C. Marshall and Geoffrey May, *The Divorce Court* (Baltimore: The Johns Hopkins Press, 1932), Vol. II, pp. 55 56.
12. The names were taken from the court calendars published in the *New York Law Journal.* The general characteristics of the sample are presented in Appendix A.
13. The only serious resistance was in response to a query about the informants' annual income. Only two of the first dozen lawyers interviewed gave an estimate of their yearly income from practice. The question was not asked in subsequent interviews. For a discussion of some of the more general problems encountered in conducting these interviews, see Appendix B.

Chapter 2

1. A. L. Kroeber and Talcott Parsons, "The Concepts of Culture and of Social System," *American Sociological Review,* XXIII (October, 1958), 583. Essentially the same distinction has been made by Sorokin. See, for example, Pitirim A. Sorokin, *Society, Culture, and Personality* (New York: Harper and Bros., 1947).
2. Our use of the concept of cultural context follows Malinowski's who defines it as "life situations which call for a given rule, the manner in which this is handled by the people concerned, the reaction of the community at large, and the consequences of fulfillment or neglect." Bronislaw Malinowski, *Crime and Custom in Savage Society* (New York: The Humanities Press, Inc., 1951), p. 125.
3. New York Civil Practice Act, Sections 1147 and 1161; and New York Domestic Relations Law, Sections 7 and 7a.
4. The divorce laws of the United States are summarized in Harriet F. Pilpel and Theodora Zavin, *Your Marriage and the Law* (New York: Rinehart and Co., 1952), 356–57; Albert C. Jacobs and Julius Goebel, Jr., *Cases and Other Materials on Domestic Relations,* 3rd ed. (New York: The Foundation Press, 1952), pp. 1102–1117.
5. Robert Kingsley, "What Are the Proper Grounds for Granting Annulments?" *Law and Contemporary Problems,* XVIII (Winter, 1953), 47.
6. Gellhorn, *op. cit.,* p. 271. For a brief history of the New York rule concerning annulment for fraud, see Harold L. Twiss, Jr., "Annulments for Fraud in New York," *Albany Law Review,* XXIV (1960), 125–35.
7. U.S. Bureau of Census, *U.S. Census of Population:* 1950, Vol. II, *Characteristics of the Population,* Part 1, "United States Summary," pp. 179–80.
8. *Ibid.,* Part 32, "New York," p. 200.
9. Jacobson, *op. cit.,* pp. 112–13.
10. *Ibid.*
11. *Ibid.,* pp. 113–14.
12. *Ibid.*
13. Alfred Cahen, *Statistical Analysis of American Divorce* (New York: Columbia University Press, 1932), p. 68.
14. Jacobson, *op. cit.,* p. 116.

15. *Ibid.*, p. 118.
16. Ploscowe, *op. cit.*, pp. 1–2.
17. Max Lerner, *America As a Civilization* (New York: Simon and Schuster, 1957), pp. 597–98.
18. Marvin B. Sussman, *Sourcebook in Marriage and the Family* (New York: Houghton Mifflin, 1955), p. 367.
19. James H. Barnett and Rhoda Gruen, "Recent American Divorce Novels, 1938–1945," *Social Forces,* XXVI (March, 1948), 322–27; James H. Barnett, *Divorce and the American Divorce Novel, 1858–1937* (Philadelphia, privately printed, 1939); Hornell Hart, "Changing Social Attitudes and Interests," in *Recent Social Trends* (New York: McGraw-Hill, 1934), pp. 382–442, especially pp. 416–17.
20. William S. Bernard, "Student Attitudes on Marriage and the Family," *American Sociological Review,* III (June, 1938), 354–61; Theodore Newcomb, "Recent Changes in Attitude toward Sex and Marriage," *American Sociological Review,* II (October, 1937), 659–67; Walter Buck, "A Measurement of Changes in Attitudes and Interests of University Students over a Ten-Year Period," *Journal of Abnormal and Social Psychology,* XXXI (April–June, 1936), 12–19.
21. Hadley Cantril (ed.), *Public Opinion: 1935–1946* (Princeton: Princeton University Press, 1951), pp. 171–72.
22. Emily Post, *Etiquette: The Blue Book of Social Usage* (New York: Funk and Wagnalls Co., 1928), p. 639; Emily Post, *Etiquette* (New York: Funk and Wagnalls Co., 1955), pp. 628 and 225.
23. Erik Allardt, "The Influence of Different Systems of Social Norms on Divorce Rates in Finland," *Marriage and Family Living,* XVII (November, 1955), 325–31.
24. Goode, *op. cit.*, p. 170.
25. Cantril, *op. cit.*
26. *Ibid.*
27. Malinowski, *op. cit.*, p. 127
28. Harry C. Harmsworth and Mhyra S. Minnis, "Non-Statutory Causes of Divorce: The Lawyer's Point of View," *Marriage and Family Living,* XVII (November, 1955), 316–21; George Squire, "The Shift from Adversary to Administrative Divorce," *Boston University Law Review,* XXXIII (April, 1953), 141–75; J. C. Fleming, "Evasion of Law and Divorce Adjudication," *International and Comparative Law Quarterly,* I (July, 1952), 381–90; Max Rheinstein, "Trends in Marriage and Divorce Law of Western Countries," *Law and Contemporary*

Problems, XVIII (Winter, 1953), 3–19; Morris Ploscowe, "The Failure of Divorce Reform," *Ohio State Law Journal,* XIII (Winter, 1952), 3–12; Reginald Heber Smith, "Dishonest Divorce," *Atlantic Monthly,* CLXXX (December, 1947), 42–45.

29. See the sources cited in the preceding footnote for evidence on each of these four patterns.

30. *The Autobiography of Lincoln Steffens* (New York: The Literary Guild, 1931). Steffens was, of course, primarily concerned with political corruption in American life, but many of his perceptive observations apply to other forms of social deviance. For current sociological views of institutionalized evasion of norms, see Merton, *Social Theory and Social Structure, op. cit.,* pp. 317–18; Robert K. Merton, "Discrimination and the American Creed," in Robert M. MacIver (ed.), *Discrimination and National Welfare* (New York: Harper and Bros., 1949), pp. 99–126; Robin M. Williams, Jr., *American Society* (New York: Alfred A. Knopf, 1956), Chap. X. That it is not easy to maintain a sociological perspective on deviance, even when one is committed to such a perspective, is illustrated by the conclusion drawn by one sociologist with an acknowledged intellectual debt to Steffens. In the course of his discussion of political machines, Chapin writes: "The problem of political corruption has its roots deep in human nature. At the very center of the problem lies the question of personality; *for the integration of the personality holds the key for solving the problem.*" [Emphasis added.] See F. Stuart Chapin, *Contemporary American Institutions* (New York: Harper and Bros., 1935), p. 44.

31. Merton, *Social Theory and Social Structure, op. cit.,* p. 73.

32. Jacobson, *op. cit.,* p. 115.

33. Alexander Lindey, "Foreign Divorces: Where Do We Go From Here?" *The University of Pittsburgh Law Review,* XVII (Winter, 1956), 149–50.

34. Goode, *op. cit.,* pp. 43–68; Thomas P. Monohan, "Divorce by Occupational Level," *Marriage and Family Living,* XVII (November, 1955), 322–24.

35. Cited by Gellhorn, *op. cit.,* p. 286; see also "Note—Collusion and Consensual Divorces and the New York Anomaly," *Columbia Law Review,* XXXVI (1936), 1121–1133.

36. Gellhorn, *op. cit.,* p. 285.

37. Jacobson, *op. cit.,* pp. 115–16.

38. Gellhorn, *op. cit.,* p. 290.

39. *Ibid.,* pp. 290–91; Richard H. Wels, "New York: The Poor

Man's Reno," *Cornell Law Quarterly,* XXXV (1950), 303–26, especially 319–21; William M. Wherry, "Changing Concepts of Law," *Bar Bulletin,* IV (March, 1949), 11; "Comment, Annulments for Fraud—New York's Answer to Reno?" *Columbia Law Review,* XLVIII (1948), 900–20.

40. Smith, *op. cit.,* p. 43.
41. Joseph N. Ulman, *A Judge Takes the Stand* (New York: Alfred A. Knopf, 1936), p. 173.
42. Ploscowe, "The Failure of Divorce Reform," *op. cit.,* p. 3.
43. *Report of the Special Committee on the Improvement of the Divorce Laws* (New York: The Association of the Bar of the City of New York, 1950), 1.
44. James S. Plant, *Personality and the Cultural Pattern* (New York: The Commonwealth Fund, 1937), p. 248, cited by Merton, *Social Theory and Social Structure, op. cit.,* p. 132.
45. The relationship between pluralistic ignorance and lawyers' knowledge of illegal behavior in matrimonial cases was drawn to my attention by Professor Robert K. Merton. Some indication of judicial recognition and acceptance of this deviance is found in Bernard Botein, *Trial Judge* (New York: Simon and Schuster, 1952), pp. 290 and 300; see also Ulman, *op. cit.,* pp. 168–75.
46. *Complete Prose Works of John Milton,* Ernest Sirluck (ed.) (New Haven: Yale University Press, 1959), Vol. II, p. 588. Contemporary divorce law, observes Judge Ulman, is "a tool of society which actually works much better than one has a right to expect of it. That is because modern judges have imitated the ancient practice which has served frequently throughout the centuries as a means to develop our legal system. They have shut their eyes in some directions, while in other directions they have been astute to see the invisible. In that way judges have created a legal fiction, by means of which a legal tool carves out socially desirable products, secures those results which society demands, without seeming to do so, sometimes pretending even that it does not do so." Ulman, *op. cit.,* p. 173.
47. Smith, *op. cit.,* p. 43.
48. Ploscowe, "The Failure of Divorce Reform," *op. cit.,* p. 3.
49. The following discussion of status and role-sets is based on Merton, *Social Theory and Social Structure, op. cit.,* pp. 368–70. Cf. Talcott Parsons, *The Social System* (Glencoe, Ill.: The Free Press, 1951), pp. 280–83.

50. *Ibid.*, p. 280. For a more general discussion of the mechanisms that reduce role conflict, see William J. Goode, "A Theory of Role Strain," *American Sociological Review,* XXV (August, 1960), 483–96; and Merton, *Social Theory and Social Structure, op. cit.,* pp. 371–80.

Chapter 3

1. For example, Robert Gerald Storey, *Professional Leadership* (Claremont, California: Claremont College, 1958); Robert Moore Fisher (ed.), *The Metropolis in Modern Life* (New York: Doubleday and Co., 1955), pp. 277–314; Elliott Dunlap Smith (ed.), *Education for Professional Responsibility* (Pittsburgh: Carnegie Press, 1948).
2. See *The 1958 Distribution of Lawyers in the United States, op. cit.,* pp. 6, 48–49; Albert Blaustein and Howard S. Kaplan, "New York Lawyer Statistics," *Bar Bulletin,* VIII (May, 1950), 26–30; Edward F. Dennison, "Incomes in Selected Professions: Part 2, Legal Services," *Survey of Current Business,* XXIII (August, 1943), 24; William Weinfeld, "Income of Lawyers, 1929–48," *Survey of Current Business,* XXIX (August, 1949), 22; Maurice Liebenberg, "Income of Lawyers in the Post-War Years," *Survey of Current Business,* XXXVI (December, 1956), 33.
3. Leonard Kent, "Economic Status of the Legal Profession in Chicago," *Illinois Law Review,* XLV (July–August, 1950), 311–32, especially 328, 331.
4. Albert Blaustein, "NYCLA—Giant of Bar Associations," *Bar Bulletin,* IX (May, 1951), 11.
5. Harrison Tweed, *The Changing Practice of Law* (New York: The Association of the Bar of the City of New York, 1955); Zechariah Chaffee, Jr., "Changes in the Law during Forty Years," *Boston University Law Review,* XXXII (January, 1952), 46–53; James Willard Hurst, *The Growth of American Law* (Boston: Little, Brown and Co., 1950), pp. 309–11; Kent, *op. cit.,* p. 326; Karl N. Llewellyn, "The Bar Specializes—With What Results?" *The Annals,* CLXVII (May, 1933), 178–90.
6. On group practice, see Roger B. Siddall, "Group Practice of Law," in *The Practical Lawyer's Law Office Manual No. 2* (Philadelphia: The Practical Lawyer, 1959), 74–79, and Joseph H. Hinshaw, "Practice in Groups," *Case and Comment,* LVII (March–April, 1952), 32–34. For data on the number of law-

yers practicing alone or in groups, see *The 1958 Distribution of Lawyers, op. cit.,* and Liebenberg, *op. cit.,* pp. 30 and 33.

7. Descriptions of various aspects of practice in large law firms can be found in Edwin C. Austin, "Some Comments on Large Law Firms," *The Practical Lawyer's Law Office Manual No. 2, op. cit.,* pp. 65–73; Elliott C. Cheatham, *Cases and Materials on the Legal Profession* (2d ed.; New York: The Foundation Press, 1955), pp. 50–54; Hurst, *op. cit.,* pp. 306–08; and Ferdinand Lundberg, "The Law Factories," *Harper's Magazine,* CLXXIX (July, 1939), 180–92.
8. For an excellent account of the emergence of these attributes in a small law firm, see Emily P. Dodge, "Evolution of a City Law Office: Part I—Office Organization," *Wisconsin Law Review* (March, 1955), 180–207; and "Evolution of a City Law Office: Part II—Office Flow of Business," *Wisconsin Law Review* (January, 1956), 35–56.
9. Emery A. Brownell, *Legal Aid in the United States* (Rochester: The Lawyers Co-operative Publishing Co., 1951), p. 209.
10. Liebenberg, *op. cit.,* p. 30; Kent, *op. cit.,* pp. 325–26, 328.
11. Weinfeld, *op. cit.;* Liebenberg, *op. cit.,* pp. 27–28, 30.
12. Maurice Rubin, "Specialization—the Grief and the Glory," *Brooklyn Barrister,* IV (January, 1953), 91–95.
13. On competition in the legal profession, see Robert Szold, "The Practice of Law as a Career," *American Bar Association Journal,* XLVI (March, 1960), 261–62; Wagner Thielens, Jr., "Some Comparisons of Entrants to Medical and Law Schools," in Robert K. Merton, George G. Reader, and Patricia L. Kendall (eds.), *The Student Physician* (Cambridge: Harvard University Press, 1957), pp. 143–52; Tweed, *op. cit.,* p. 29; David Riesman, *Individualism Reconsidered* (Glencoe, Ill.: The Free Press, 1954), pp. 452–57; Charles B. Stephens, "Finding Your Place in the Legal Profession," in Arthur T. Vanderbilt (ed.), *Studying Law* (New York: Washington Square Publishing Corporation, 1945), p. 698.
14. Cheatham, *op. cit.,* pp. 461–86; Albert P. Blaustein and Charles O. Porter, *The American Lawyer* (Chicago: University of Chicago Press, 1954), pp. 126–29; Hurst, *op. cit.,* pp. 319–22.
15. See, for example, the conclusions reached in the *Survey of the Legal Profession in New York County* (New York: Committee on Professional Economics of the New York County Lawers Association, 1936), p. 58. See also *The Economics of the Legal Profession* (Chicago: American Bar Association, 1938), pp. 58–68; and Young B. Smith and James Grafton Rogers, "The

Overcrowding of the Bar and What Can Be Done About It," *American Law School Review,* VII (December, 1932), 565–76.

16. Recent trends in legal incomes and numbers of law school students are discussed in *Lawyers' Economic Problems and Some Bar Association Solutions* (Chicago: American Bar Association, Economics of Law Practice Series, Number Two, n.d.).
17. The concepts of latent and manifest identities are discussed in Alvin W. Gouldner, "Cosmopolitans and Locals: Toward an Analysis of Latent Social Roles—I," *Administrative Science Quarterly,* II (December, 1957), 281–306.
18. Dan C. Lortie, "Laymen to Lawmen: Law School, Careers, and Professional Socialization," *Harvard Educational Review,* XXIX (Fall, 1959), 352–69.
19. *Ibid.*, pp. 357–60.
20. The effects of discrimination on legal careers has yet to be studied systematically. Some evidence and discussion of the problem may be found in Louis A. Toepfer, "Placement in the Legal Profession," *American Bar Association Journal,* XXXVII (July, 1951), 497–501, 555–60; Erwin O. Smigel, "The Impact of Recruitment on the Organization of the Large Law Firm," *American Sociological Review,* XXV (February, 1960), 56–66; Spencer Klaw, "The Wall Street Lawyer," *Fortune,* LIX (February, 1958), 140, 141–44, 192, 194, 197–98, 202; Melvin Fagen, "The Status of Jewish Lawyers in New York," *Jewish Social Studies,* I (1939), 73–104; William Henri Hale, *The Career Development of the Negro Lawyer in Chicago* (unpublished Ph.D. dissertation, Department of Sociology, University of Chicago, 1949); Blaustein and Porter, *op. cit.,* pp. 29–32.
21. Blaustein and Porter, *op. cit.,* pp. 29–32 and 197; Fagan, *op. cit.,* pp. 100–103; Hale, *op. cit.,* pp. 71–73; Smigel, *op. cit.,* p. 58.
22. Frederick H. Jackson, *Simeon Eben Baldwin: Lawyer, Social Scientist, Statesman* (New York: Columbia University Press, 1955); George Wharton Pepper, *Philadelphia Lawyer: An Autobiography* (New York: J. B. Lippincott Co., 1944); Arthur Mann, *La Guardia: A Fighter Against His Times, 1882–1933* (New York: J. B. Lippincott Co., 1959); Louis Waldman, *Labor Lawyer* (New York: E. P. Dutton and Co., 1944). For a discussion of the influence of nontechnical, or latent, attributes in medical practice, see Oswald Hall's articles: "Types of Medical Careers," *op. cit.,* and "The Stages of a Medical Career," *op. cit.* See, in addition, Lieberson, *op. cit.* For a study of the effects of such attributes on the careers of factory mana-

gers, see Melville Dalton, "Informal Factors in Career Achievement," *American Journal of Sociology,* LVI (March, 1951), 407–15.

23. For example, Harold P. Seligson, *Building a Practice* (rev. ed.; New York: Practicing Law Institute, 1953), pp. 3–7; James R. Richardson, *Establishing a Law Practice* (Rochester: The Lawyers Co-operative Publishing Co., 1958), Chap. V; John E. Tracy, *The Successful Practice of Law* (New York: Prentice-Hall, Inc., 1947), Chap. I; Claude R. Miller, *Practice of Law* (Chicago: Callaghan and Co., 1946), Chap. IV.
24. Karl N. Llewellyn, "Where Do We Go From Here?" *American Law School Review,* VII (April, 1934), 1038.
25. Shosteck found, in his study of over 2000 law school graduates, that scholastic standing and type of initial employment were related. Graduates in the top third of their class were more likely than others to become salaried associates in law firms; those in the bottom third of their class were more apt than others to enter practice by themselves. See Robert Shosteck, *Report of Follow-Up Study of Economic Status of Law Graduates of 1946 and 1947* (Washington, D.C.: B'nai B'rith Vocational Service Bureau, 1950, mimeographed), 18.
26. There is some indication that the currently high demand for legal talent is weakening the discriminatory hiring practices of large law firms. See Smigel, *op. cit.,* p. 59.
27. An earlier study reported that almost eight out of ten Jewish attorneys in group practice in New York City were in law firms staffed primarily by other Jewish lawyers. Fagen *op. cit.,* p. 103. Since data on the religious affiliation of our informants' partners were not obtained directly, the finding about this sample must be considered as a crude approximation. Firms were classified as Jewish if more than half of the partners had stereotyped Jewish surnames. The data, therefore, probably underestimate the number of informants in Jewish firms.
28. The low demand is related to the relative scarcity of Negro businessmen, the high proportion of Negroes with low incomes, and the tendency for many Negroes to believe that their interests can be better served through hiring white lawyers. The concern of Negro lawyers for independence derives from a desire to be less dependent on the white community for employment. See Hale, *op. cit.,* and G. Franklin Edwards, *The Negro Professional Class* (Glencoe, Ill.: The Free Press, 1959).
29. Eugene C. Gerhart, *Organization of Law Practice* (Boston: Survey of the Legal Profession, 1951), p. 5.

30. Milton Terris and Mary Monk, "Changes in Physicians' Careers: Relation of Time after Graduation to Specialization," in E. Gartly Jaco (ed.), *Patients, Physicians and Illness* (Glencoe, Ill.: The Free Press, 1958), pp. 361–65; H. G. Weiskotten and Marion E. Altenderfer, "Trends in Medical Practice," *Journal of Medical Education,* XXXI (July, 1956), 8.
31. Albert J. Harno, *Legal Education in the United States* (San Francisco: Bancroft-Whitney Co., 1953), pp. 148–55.
32. For illustrations of this effect of a "big case," see Martin W. Littleton, *My Partner-in-Law: The Life of George Martin Levy* (New York: Farrar, Straus and Cudahy, 1957), pp. 25–30; John W. Noble and Bernard Averbuch, *Never Plead Guilty: The Story of Jake Ehrlich* (New York: Farrar, Straus and Cudahy, 1955), pp. 38–50. A "big case" has the additional effect of making a lawyer's legal ability more salient to others than his nonprofessional statuses. For example, a woman lawyer's participation in a publicized murder trial may lessen the significance of her sex status in professional work. For a case in point, see Tierra Farrow's autobiography, *Lawyer in Petticoats* (New York: Vantage Press, 1953), Chaps. XV–XVI, and p. 112.
33. Shosteck, *op. cit.,* p. 22.
34. Lortie, *op. cit.,* pp. 357–60.
35. For evidence on the effects of these variables in the field of medicine, particularly with reference to public health programs, see George M. Foster, *Problems in Intercultural Health Programs* (New York: Social Science Research Council Pamphlet No. 12, 1958); Ozzie G. Simmons, *Social Status and Public Health* (New York: Social Science Research Council Pamphlet, No. 13, 1958); Benjamin D. Paul (ed.), *Health, Culture, and Community* (New York: Russell Sage Foundation, 1955); Earl L. Koos, *The Health of Regionville* (New York: Columbia University Press, 1954); Lyle Saunders, *Cultural Differences and Medical Care* (New York: Russell Sage Foundation, 1954).
36. Earl L. Koos, *The Family and the Law* (Boston: Survey of the Legal Profession, 1948, mimeographed); Charles E. Clark and Emma Corstvet, "The Lawyer and the Public," *Yale Law Journal,* XLVII (1938), 1272–1293. Cf. George Buckner, 2nd, "What Your Clients Think of You," *Journal of the Missouri Bar,* XVII (November, 1961), 468–471, 478–485. The exact nature of the relationship between class background and the use of professional legal help is far from clear. Undoubtedly, the relationship varies by type of legal action. More impor-

tantly, it is affected by three prior decisions: (a) the recognition of a legal problem; (b) the conviction that something can be done to resolve the problem; and (c) the belief that a lawyer is the person most likely to be helpful in solving the problem. The complexity of the effects of class position on decisions to seek legal counsel is illustrated by findings from Hunting and Neuwirth's study of automobile accident claims. Generally, the study reports, the lower an individual's socio-economic status, the less likely he is to take action as a result of his injury. However, among those who decide to take action, individuals with low socio-economic status are more likely to employ a lawyer than those with high socio-economic status who are more apt to press their claims themselves. See Roger Bryant Hunting and Gloria S. Neuwirth, *Who Sues in New York City?* (New York: Columbia University Press, 1962), pp. 98–100.

37. Koos, *The Family and the Law, op. cit.*
38. For evidence on the different attitudes of various strata toward professionals, see *Lay Opinion of Iowa Lawyers, Courts, and Laws* (Des Moines: The Iowa State Bar Association, 1949); Koos, *The Health of Regionville, op. cit.;* Frederic W. Terrien, "Who Thinks What about Educators?" *American Journal of Sociology,* LIX (September, 1953), 150–58; August B. Hollingshead and Frederick C. Redlich, *Social Class and Mental Illness* (New York: John Wiley and Sons, Inc., 1958), Chap. XI.
39. Reginald Heber Smith, *Justice and the Poor* (New York: The Carnegie Foundation for the Advancement of Teaching, Bulletin No. 13, 1919). See also Blaustein and Porter, *op. cit.,* p. 65, and Brownell, *op. cit., passim.*

Chapter 4

1. Each interview protocol was examined in order to ascertain how central, in the informant's opinion, matrimonial cases were to his practice. Three prevailing judgments were found: (1) the cases were perceived as *peripheral* to practice; (2) the cases were perceived as having a definite but *minor* place in practice; (3) the cases were seen as a *major* part of practice. The typology of matrimonial practice is based on these judgments supplied by our informants.
2. There are two reasons why estimates of the annual number of matrimonial clients should be used cautiously, preferably in

conjunction with other kinds of data. First, in some practices, the number of such clients varies considerably from year to year. Second, although the estimate would appear to be more useful if incorporated into a ratio based on all annual clients, the fact that some clienteles are permanent and others transitory makes comparisons difficult to interpret. These same two problems are encountered in any attempt to assess estimates of the proportion of time devoted by lawyers to particular types of legal problems.

3. The total responses exceed eighteen because several informants cited more than one major referral source.
4. Lawyers who gave this answer usually insisted that the problem of which jurisdiction to use varied with the circumstances surrounding each case; therefore, no generalizations were possible.
5. One informant, who appeared annoyed by the question, replied by saying: "I can't advise my client to evade the local jurisdiction." This position is curious in the light of rulings to the contrary by local bar committees on professional ethics. See, for example, *Opinions of the Committees on Professional Ethics of the Association of the Bar of the City of New York and the New York County Lawyers' Association* (New York: Columbia University Press, 1956), pp. 355–56, 695–96.

Chapter 5

1. On the emotionalism of matrimonial clients, see Kargman, *op. cit.*, p. 399; Ehrlich, *op. cit.*, p. 365; and Spellman, *op. cit.*, pp. 1–2.
2. This is not to say that emotionalism is inevitably present in matrimonial cases, or that it is confined to these cases. Certainly there is some unknown, though probably small, proportion of marital clients who manifest little psychic distress. The relative calmness of these latter clients was mentioned by lawyers, but usually as being atypical. In the words of one informant: "There are some exceptions like the young lady in here recently who just coolly calculated what was the best thing for her. Most of them are quite upset."
3. See, for example, the discussion of "basic adjustive techniques" in Norman Cameron, *The Psychology of Behavior Disorders* (New York: Houghton Mifflin Co., 1947), Chap. VI.

4. John Sirjamaki, *The American Family in the Twentieth Century* (Cambridge: Harvard University Press, 1953), pp. 167–71; Ernest W. Burgess and Harvey J. Locke, *The Family: From Institution to Companionship* (New York: American Book Co., 2d ed., 1953), pp. 581–93; Waller, *op. cit.*, pp. 513–27; Robert A. Harper, *Marriage* (New York: Appleton Century Crofts, 1949), pp. 234–35; Meyer F. Nimkoff, *Marriage and the Family* (New York: Houghton Mifflin and Co., 1947), pp. 639–40; Ray Baber, *Marriage and the Family* (New York: McGraw-Hill Book Co., 1939), p. 484. For empirical evidence on personal disturbance during the process of divorce, see Goode, *op. cit.,* pp. 184–201.
5. Merton, *op. cit.,* p. 295. For a more general analysis of compulsive alienation, see Talcott Parsons, *The Social System* (Glencoe, Ill.: The Free Press, 1951), p. 255.
6. Louis Nizer, "Psychological Insights in the Practice of Law," *Brooklyn Law Review,* XXV (April, 1959), 217–30; and Spellman, *op. cit.,* Chap. I.
7. Commenting on this norm, Judge Samuel Hofstader writes: "It results in a stream of vituperation and recrimination. Every incident is magnified; every quarrel an assault. The wife depicts the husband as a savage riddled with vices; the husband portrays her as a neglectful mother and a slovenly housekeeper. The charges and countercharges freeze into a permanent attitude of hostility." See his opinion in *Palmieri v. Palmieri, New York Law Journal,* 138 (November 18, 1957), 2.
8. Merton, *op. cit.,* pp. 197–200; Kenneth Burke, *Permanence and Change* (rev. ed.; Los Altos, California: Hermes Publication, 1954), Chap. III.
9. The study, directed by Star for the National Opinion Research Council and based on interviews with 3500 persons representing a sample of the adult American public, was designed to describe popular conceptions of mental illness. See Shirley A. Star, *The Dilemma of Mental Illness* (forthcoming). For a preliminary report, see Star's remarks published in *Psychiatry, the Press and the Public* (Washington, D.C.: The American Psychiatric Association, 1956), p. 3.
10. "It is not enough," notes Spellman, "to apply the usual methods of daily practice to marital litigation. . . . The standard equipment and skills of a lawyer must be augmented by a separate and additional group of techniques." Spellman, *op. cit.,* p. 1. That attorneys might be better able to represent matrimonial clients if they were formally taught to cope with emotional problems seems evident. Whether they should, and

given the demands put on the modern legal curriculum, whether they can be so trained, are questions that go beyond the scope of this monograph. For a brief statement of the problem, see Kenneth Reddon, "Domestic Relations—Stepchild of the Curriculum," *Journal of Legal Education,* VI 1953–1954), 82–84.

In general, very few law schools have attempted to incorporate any of the behavioral sciences into their curricula. For example, a survey of the 128 law schools approved by the American Bar Association revealed that, in 1957, only 25 per cent of them offered courses in either psychiatry or psychology. Furthermore, about one-fourth of the law school deans stated their belief that such courses should not be included in a legal curriculum. See John M. MacDonald, "The Teaching of Psychiatry in Law Schools," *The Journal of Criminal Law, Criminology, and Police Science,* XLIX (November–December, 1958), 310–15.

11. A context approximated, perhaps, only in the contest of a will, where, as an informant told us, "you can have just as much acrimony. . . . Quarrelling over a will may put brother against sister or children against parents." Cf. Eric A. Plaut, "Emotional Aspects of Probate Practice," *The Practical Lawyer,* V (December, 1959), 17–27.
12. Cheatham, *op. cit.,* Chaps. III–VII; and Henry S. Drinker, *Legal Ethics* (New York: Columbia University Press, 1953).
13. For a general discussion of public and professional judgments of professional competence, see William J. Goode, "Community within a Community: The Professions," *American Sociological Review,* XXII (April, 1957), 194–200. See also the relevant comments on the social consequences of ignorance in Wilbert E. Moore and Melvin M. Tumin, "Some Social Functions of Ignorance," *American Sociological Review,* XIV (December, 1949), 787–95.
14. Ehrlich also cites this attribute as characteristic of matrimonial clients. Ehrlich, *op. cit.,* pp. 362–63.
15. See, for example, Goode, *After Divorce, op. cit.,* p. 29; and Baber, *op. cit.,* pp. 484–85.
16. As Goode points out, the position of the ex-wife is likely to be more ambiguous than the ex-husband's. Goode, *After Divorce, op. cit.,* pp. 12–15.
17. This attribute is also mentioned by Nizer, *op. cit.,* pp. 221–23; and Spellman, *op. cit.,* pp. 4, 14, 72.
18. Legally, an alimony award is not simply an enforcement of the husband's duty to support his ex-wife. The purpose of an

alimony decree, as Jacobs and Goebel note, "is to convert what had theretofore been an obligation of support attaching to the status as a matter of general law into an obligation which depends on judicial fiat." Albert C. Jacobs and Julius Goebel, Jr., *Cases and Other Materials on Domestic Relations* (New York: The Foundation Press, 3rd ed., 1952), p. 818.

19. In New York County, during the year ended June 30, 1952, there were about 400 applications for temporary alimony submitted to the Court. During the same period 271 applications were made to punish for contempt those who had defaulted in alimony payments. Gellhorn, *op. cit.,* p. 343.
20. In most cases the husband is not sent to jail. "The standard practice," writes Gellhorn, ". . . is to fine the delinquent husband the amount of arrears, allowing him to purge himself by paying off the arrears in weekly instalments, and authorizing a commitment order to issue without further notice if there is any subsequent default." *Ibid.,* p. 344.
21. In the words of Curtis: "He must keep as far away as he must, and as close as he dares. He must keep his head in his case and his heart out of it; for in a paradoxical way, only by withholding some of himself can he give his client the best of himself." Charles P. Curtis, "The General Practitioner and the Specialist," in *Conference on the Profession of Law and Legal Education* (Chicago: University of Chicago Law School, 1952), pp. 5–6.
22. "Until you have represented a matrimonial cause," observes Spellman, "you have no real measure of the irritation to which a lawyer can be subjected." *Op cit.,* p. 2.
23. Strain was also the reason cited most frequently by different types of matrimonial practitioners. In addition to emotional strain, 26 per cent claimed that some lawyers do not have the time to take matrimonial cases, 26 per cent believed that the cases are avoided because they are considered unremunerative, and 14 per cent noted that certain attorneys reject the cases for religious reasons.

Chapter 6

1. Wilensky, *op. cit.,* p. 112.
2. James Coleman, Elihu Katz, and Herbert Menzel, "The Diffusion of an Innovation among Physicians," *Sociometry,* XX (December, 1957), 253–69; Herbert Menzel and Elihu Katz, "Social Relations and Innovations in the Medical Profession," *Public Opinion Quarterly,* XIX (1956), 337–52.

3. Ithiel de Sola Pool and Irwin Shulman, "Newsmen's Fantasies, Audiences, and Newswriting," *Public Opinion Quarterly,* XXIII (Summer, 1959), 145–58.
4. Wilensky, *op. cit.,* Chaps. VII and VIII; Lazarsfeld and Thielens, *op. cit.,* pp. 140–41; Pelz, *op. cit.;* Reissman, *op. cit.*
5. The analysis of role orientations is based on the responses of sixty-nine informants. Since thirteen informants reported no preferences or dissatisfactions in law practice, they could not be coded by role orientation. The lawyers were asked to describe the the "most satisfying" and "least satisfying" parts of their practices.
6. See, for example, Ronald J. Pelligrin and Charles H. Coates, "Executives and Supervisors: Contrasting Definitions of Career Success," *Administrative Science Quarterly,* I (December, 1956), 506–17; Nancy C. Morse and Robert S. Weiss, "The Functions and Meaning of Work and the Job," *American Sociological Review,* XX (April, 1955), 191–98; Elizabeth L. Lyman, "Occupational Differences in the Value Attached to Work," *American Journal of Sociology,* LXI (September, 1955), 138–44; Milton Friedman and Simon Kuznets, *Income from Professional Independent Practice* (New York: National Bureau of Economic Research, 1945), p. 130 and *passim.*
7. Morris Rosenberg, *Occupation and Values* (Glencoe, Ill.: The Free Press, 1957), pp. 11–13, 17–19.
8. William M. Kaplan, "Forgotten Canons," *New York University Law Review,* XXXIII (May, 1958), 652–65; Alexander L. Schlosser, *Lawyers Must Eat* (New York: The Vanguard Press, 1933), p. 116.
9. Drinker, *Legal Ethics, op. cit.,* Chap. VI, especially pp. 122–28, 142–48; Cheatham, *op. cit.,* pp. 144–46.
10. Cf. Lauren G. Wispe and Kenneth E. Lloyd, "Some Situational and Psychological Determinants of the Desire for Structured Interpersonal Relations," *Journal of Abnormal and Social Psychology,* LI (1955), 57–60.
11. Blaustein and Porter, *op. cit.,* pp. 119–23.
12. *Ibid.,* p. 121.
13. Paul A. Alexander, "The Family Court—An Obstacle Race," *University of Pittsburgh Law Review,* XIX (Spring, 1958), 609.
14. Glenn McCracken, Jr., "Note—The Role of the Lawyer in Divorce: Some Ethical Problems," *University of Pittsburgh Law Review,* XXI (June, 1960), 720–730; Marie W. Kargman, "The Lawyer's Role in Divorce Reconciliation," *The Practical Lawyer,* VI (March, 1960), 21–31.

15. Alexander, *op. cit.,* p. 607; Morris L. Ernst and David Loth, *For Better or Worse* (New York: Harper and Bros., 1951), p. 215.
16. In its Opinion 82, The American Bar Association's Committee on Professional Ethics and Grievances held that "in many divorse cases the best interests of both parties will be promoted by a reconciliation; but in other cases the best interests of one or the other or even of both parties will be promoted by the divorce. If the attorney honestly believed that the best interests of his client would be prejudiced by a reconciliation, it was, in the opinion of the committee entirely proper for him to advise his client to that effect." *Opinions of the Committee on Professional Ethics and Grievances* (Chicago: American Bar Association, 1947), p. 191. See also Spellman, *op. cit.,* p. 96.
17. See Richard H. Wels' remarks in "The Lawyer as a Family Counselor," *op. cit.,* p. 49.
18. Ehrlich, *op. cit.,* pp. 362–63.
19. Merton, *Social Theory and Social Structure, op. cit.,* p. 423.
20. For provisional data on the number of reconciliations effected in the Conciliation Court of Los Angeles, see Gellhorn, *op. cit.,* pp. 373–74. Cf. Quintin Johnstone, "Divorce Dismissals: A Field Study," *Kansas Law Review,* I (May, 1953), 245–57.

SELECTED BIBLIOGRAPHY

Books

Barnett, James H. *Divorce and the American Divorce Novel, 1858–1937*. Philadelphia, 1939. (privately printed.)

Blaustein, Albert P., and Porter, Charles O. *The American Lawyer*. Chicago: University of Chicago Press, 1954.

Brownell, Emery A. *Legal Aid in the United States*. Rochester: The Lawyers Co-operative Publishing Co., 1951.

Cahen, Alfred. *Statistical Analysis of American Divorce*. New York: Columbia University Press, 1932.

Cantril, Hadley (ed.). *Public Opinion: 1935–1946*. Princeton, N.J.: Princeton University Press, 1951.

Caplow, Theodore. *The Sociology of Work*. Minneapolis: University of Minnesota Press, 1954.

Carlin, Jerome E. *Lawyers on Their Own*. New Brunswick, N.J.: Rutgers University Press, 1962.

Carr-Saunders, A. M., and Wilson, P. A. *The Professions*. London: Oxford University Press, 1933.

Cheatham, Elliott E. *Cases and Materials on the Legal Profession*. New York: The Foundation Press, second edition, 1955.

Davis, F. James, *et al*. *Society and the Law*. New York: The Free Press of Glencoe, 1962.

Dos Passos, John R. *The American Lawyer*. New York: Consolidated Law Book Co., 1919.

Drinker, Henry S. *Legal Ethics*. New York: Columbia University Press, 1953.

Evan, William M. (ed.) *Law and Sociology*. New York: The Free Press of Glencoe, 1962.

Gellhorn, Walter. *Children and Families in the Courts of New York*. New York: Dodd, Mead and Co., 1954.

Goode, William J. *After Divorce*. New York: The Free Press of Glencoe, 1956.

Harno, Albert J. *Legal Education in the United States*. San Francisco: Bancroft-Whitney Co., 1953.

Hurst, James W. *The Growth of American Law*. Boston: Little, Brown and Co., 1950.

Jacobs, Albert C., and Goebel, Julius, Jr. *Cases and Other Materials on Domestic Relations*. New York: The Foundation Press, Inc., third edition, 1952.

Jacobson, Paul H. *American Marriage and Divorce*. New York: Rinehart and Co., Inc., 1959.

Malinowski, Bronislaw. *Crime and Custom in Savage Society*. New York: The Humanities Press, 1951.

Merton, Robert K. *Social Theory and Social Structure*. New York: The Free Press of Glencoe, revised and enlarged edition, 1957.

Parsons, Talcott. *Essays in Sociological Theory*. New York: The Free Press of Glencoe, revised edition, 1954.

———. *The Social System*. New York: The Free Press of Glencoe, 1951.

Paul, Benjamin D. (ed.). *Health, Culture and Community*. New York: Russell Sage Foundation, 1955.

Pilpel, Harriet F., and Zavin, Theodora. *Your Marriage and the Law*. New York: Rinehart and Co., Inc., 1952.

Ploscowe, Morris. *The Truth About Divorce*. New York: Hawthorn Books, Inc., 1955.

Rosenberg, Morris. *Occupations and Values*. New York: The Free Press of Glencoe, 1957.

Schlosser, Alexander L. *Lawyers Must Eat*. New York: Vanguard Press, 1933.

Smith, Reginald H. *Justice and the Poor*. New York: The Carnegie Foundation for the Advancement of Teaching, Bulletin No. 13, 1919.

Sorokin, Pitirim A. *Society, Culture, and Personality*. New York: Harper and Bros., 1947.

Spellman, Howard H. *Successful Management of Matrimonial Cases*. New York: Prentice-Hall, Inc., 1954.

Virtue, Maxine. *Family Cases in Court*. Durham, N.C.: Duke University Press, 1956.

Wilensky, Harold L. *Intellectuals in Labor Unions*. New York: The Free Press of Glencoe, 1956.

Williams, Robin M., Jr. *American Society*. New York: Alfred A. Knopf, 1956.

Articles, Monographs, and Pamphlets

Allardt, Erik. "The Influence of Different Systems of Social Norms on Divorce Rates in Finland." *Marriage and Family Living*, XVII (November, 1955), 325–31.

American Bar Foundation. *The 1958 Distribution of Lawyers in the United States*. Chicago: American Bar Foundation, 1959.

Association of the Bar of the City of New York. *Report of the Special Committee of the Improvement of the Divorce Laws*. New York: The Association of the Bar of the City of New York, 1950.

Barnett, James H., and Gruen, Rhoda. "Recent American Divorce Novels, 1938–1945." *Social Forces*, XXVI (March, 1948), 322–27.

Carr-Saunders, Alexander M. "Metropolitan Conditions and Traditional Professional Relationships." In Fisher, Robert M. (ed.), *The Metropolis in Modern Life*. New York: Doubleday and Co., 1955, pp. 279–87.

Chaffee, Zechariah, Jr. "Changes in the Law During Forty Years." *Boston University Law Review*, XXXII (January, 1952), 46–53.

Clark, Charles E., and Corstvet, Emma. "The Lawyer and the Public." *Yale Law Journal*, XLVII (1938), 1272–1293.

"Comment—Annulments for Fraud—New York's Answer to Reno?" *Columbia Law Review*, XLVIII (1948), 900–20.

"Comment—Collusive and Consensual Divorce and the New York Anomaly." *Columbia Law Review*, XXXVI (1936), 1121–33.

Conference on Divorce. Chicago: The University of Chicago Law School, 1952.

Curtis, Charles P. "The General Practitioner and the Specialist." In *Conference on the Profession of Law and Legal Education*. Chicago: The University of Chicago Law School, Conference Series No. 11, 1952, pp. 3–10.

"Divorce—A Re-examination of Basic Concepts." *Law and Contemporary Problems*, XVIII (Winter, 1953).

Drinker, Henry S. "Problems of Professional Ethics in Matrimonial Litigation." *Harvard Law Review*, LXVI (January, 1953), 443–64.

Ehrlich, Stanton L. "What Is a Divorce Lawyer?" *Marriage and Family Living*, XXI (November, 1959), 361–66.

Fleming, J. G. "Evasion of Law and Divorce Adjudication." *In-*

ternational and Comparative Law Quarterly, I (July, 1952), 381–90.

Goode, William J. "A Theory of Role Strain." *American Sociological Review,* XXV (August, 1960), 483–96.

———. "Community within a Community: The Professions." *American Sociological Review,* XXII (April, 1957), 194–200.

Gouldner, Alvin W. "Organizational Analysis." In Merton, Robert K., Broom, Leonard, and Cottrell, Leonard S., Jr. (eds.), *Sociology Today.* New York: Basic Books, Inc., 1959, pp. 400–28.

———. "Cosmopolitans and Locals: Toward an Analysis of Latent Social Roles—I." *Administrative Science Quarterly,* II (December, 1957), 281–306.

Hale, William H. "The Career Development of the Negro Lawyer in Chicago." Unpublished Ph.D. dissertation, University of Chicago, 1949.

Harmsworth, Harry C., and Minnis, Mhyra S. "Non-Statutory Causes of Divorce: The Lawyer's Point of View." *Marriage and Family Living,* XVII (November, 1955), 316–21.

"Interim Report of the Special Committee on Improvement of Family Law." *The Record,* XIII (February, 1958), 98–100.

Jacobson, Paul H. "Marital Dissolutions in New York State in Relation to Their Trends in the U.S." *Milbank Memorial Fund Quarterly,* XXVIII (January, 1950), 25–42.

Kaplan, William M. "Forgotten Canons." *New York University Law Review,* XXXIII (May, 1958), 652–65.

Kargman, Marie W. "The Lawyer as Divorce Counselor." *American Bar Association Journal,* XLVI (April, 1960), pp. 399–401.

Kingsley, Robert. "What Are the Proper Grounds for Granting Annulments?" *Law and Contemporary Problems,* XVIII (Winter, 1953), 39–48.

Koos, Earl L. *The Family and the Law.* Boston: Survey of the Legal Profession, 1948. (Mimeographed.)

Kroeber, A. L., and Parsons, Talcott. "The Concepts of Culture and of Social System." *American Sociological Review,* XXIII (October, 1958), 582–83.

"The Lawyer as a Family Counselor." *The University of Kansas Law Review,* XXII (Fall, 1953), 28–53.

Lindey, Alexander. "Foreign Divorce: Where Do We Go From Here?" *The University of Pittsburgh Law Review,* XVII (Winter, 1956), 125–50.

Lortie, Dan C. "Laymen to Lawmen: Law Schools, Careers, and Professional Socialization." *Harvard Educational Review,* XXIX (Fall, 1959), 352–69.

Lyman, Elizabeth L. "Occupational Differences in the Value Attached to Work." *American Journal of Sociology,* LXI (September, 1955), 138–44.

MacDonald, John M. "The Teaching of Psychiatry in Law Schools." *Journal of Criminal Law, Criminology, and Police Science,* XLIX (November–December, 1958), pp. 310–15.

Merton, Robert K. "Discrimination and the American Creed." In MacIver, Robert M. (ed.), *Discrimination and National Welfare.* New York: Harper and Bros., 1949, pp. 99–126.

Moore, Underhill, and Sussman, Gilbert. "The Lawyer's Law." *Yale Law Review,* XLI (1931–1932), 566–76.

Morse, Nancy C., and Weiss, Robert S. "The Functions and Meaning of Work and the Job." *American Sociological Review,* XX (April, 1955), 191–98.

Nizer, Louis. "Psychological Insights in the Practice of Law." *Brooklyn Law Review,* XXV (April, 1959), 217–30.

Opinions of the Committee on Professional Ethics and Grievances. Chicago: American Bar Association, 1947.

Opinions of the Committees on Professional Ethics of the Association of the Bar of the City of New York and the New York County Lawyers Association. New York: Columbia University Press, 1956.

Ploscowe, Morris. "The Failure of Divorce Reform." *Ohio State Law Journal,* XIII (Winter, 1952), 3–12.

———. "The Confusing Problem of Jurisdiction." In *Law, Medicine and the Unstable Family.* New York: New York Lawyers Association, 1949, pp. 32–37.

Reddon, Kenneth. "Domestic Relations—Stepchild of the Curriculum." *Journal of Legal Education,* VI (1953–1954), 82–84.

Rheinstein, Max. "Trends in Marriage and Divorce Law in Western Countries." *Law and Contemporary Problems,* XVIII (Winter, 1953), 3–19.

Smigel, Erwin O. "The Impact of Recruitment on the Organization of the Large Law Firm." *American Sociological Review,* XXV (February, 1960), 56–66.

Smith, Reginald H. "Dishonest Divorce." *Atlantic Monthly,* CLXXX (December, 1947), 42–45.

Squire, George. "The Shift from Adversary to Administrative Divorce." *Boston University Law Review,* XXXIII (April, 1953), 141–75.

"Symposium on Domestic Relations." *Vanderbilt Law Review,* IX (June, 1956).

Toepfer, Louis A. "Placement in the Legal Profession." *American Bar Association Journal,* XXXVII (July, 1951), 497–501, 555–60.

Tweed, Harrison. *The Changing Practice of Law*. New York: The Association of the Bar of the City of New York, 1955.

Twiss, Harold L., Jr. "Annulments for Fraud in New York." *Albany Law Review,* XXIV (1960), 125–35.

Wels, Richard H. "New York: The Poor Man's Reno." *Cornell Law Quarterly,* XXXV (1950), 303–26.

Wispe, L. G., and Lloyd, K. E. "Some Situational and Psychological Determinants of the Desire for Structured Interpersonal Relations." *Journal of Abnormal and Social Psychology,* LI (1955), 57–60.

INDEX